Excel

ADVANCED SKILLS

ENGLISH

YEAR 4

AGES 9–10

GRAMMAR AND PUNCTUATION WORKBOOK

Get the Results You Want!

PASCAL PRESS

Laura Anderson

Reprinted 2015 (twice), 2016, 2018, 2020, 2021, 2022, 2024

ISBN 978 1 74125 400 6

Pascal Press
PO Box 250
Glebe NSW 2037
(02) 9198 1748
www.pascalpress.com.au

Publisher: Vivienne Joannou
Project editor: Mark Dixon
Edited by Leanne Howard
Reviewed by Dale Little and Kristine Brown
Cover and page design by DiZign Pty Ltd
Typeset by lj Design (Julianne Billington)
Printed by Vivar Printing/Green Giant Press

Contents

To the student ... v
About this book ... vi
Unit 1 School excursions ... 1
Recounts/emails
Sentences
Writing sentences—capital letters and full stops ... 1
Subject and verb in sentences ... 3
Unit 2 So that's how it works! ... 7
Narratives
Sentences
Statements and questions—full stops and question marks ... 7
Exclamations and commands—full stops and exclamation marks ... 9
Unit 3 Endangered animals ... 13
Information reports
Nouns
Common nouns ... 13
Proper nouns—capital letters ... 15
Unit 4 Tales from long ago ... 19
Narratives
Nouns
Collective nouns and compound nouns ... 19
Abstract nouns ... 21
Unit 5 Pirates ... 25
Website articles
Nouns
Plural nouns ... 25
Unit 6 Healthy living ... 31
Advertisements
Pronouns
Personal pronouns ... 31
Reflexive pronouns ... 31
Possessive pronouns ... 33
Interrogative pronouns ... 33
Unit 7 Wonders of the world ... 37
Descriptions
Adjectives
Descriptive adjectives ... 37
Comparing adjectives ... 39

Unit 8 The wonderful world of animation **43**
Reviews
Verbs
Doing verbs 43
Helping verbs 45

Unit 9 Festivals and holidays **49**
Diary entries
Verbs
Saying, thinking and feeling verbs 49
'Being' and 'having' verbs 51

Unit 10 Exploring the unknown **55**
Recount/Report
Present/present continuous tense 55
Past/past continuous tense 55
Future tense 57

Unit 11 Ways of communicating **61**
Explanations
Adverbs 61
Adverbial phrases 63
Prepositions 64

Unit 12 Let's get creative! **67**
Descriptions/Procedures
Adjectival phrases 67
Noun groups 69

Unit 13 The seasons **73**
Poems/Recounts
Commas and lists 73
Contractions 73
Apostrophes of omission 73
Apostrophes of possession 75

Unit 14 Being adventurous **79**
Discussions/Reports
Direct speech—speech marks 79
Reported speech 81

Unit 15 What's making news? **85**
Newspaper reports
Compound and complex sentences 85
Conjunctions 85
Relative pronouns 87

Unit 16 Secrets of the sea **91**
Narratives
Using commas in compound and complex sentences 91
Quotation marks 93
Capital letters 93

Glossary of terms **97**

Answers **99**

To the student

This book explains the rules of grammar and punctuation that you need for Year 4.

Each unit focuses on two or more grammar rules. Before each rule is explained, there is a text that lets you see how the rule works in everyday writing. These texts are important as they are models of the different text types and will help you in your own writing. There is also a short NAPLAN-style test that lets you see how well you have understood the grammar rules.

Most of the activities can be written in this book, but you will have to use your own paper for the writing activity at the end of each unit. I suggest you buy a notebook or folder for this. The writing activities are very important. The more you do, the faster your English will improve. If you are not sure how to write something, use the example texts as a model.

It is important that you work through this book from Unit 1 to the end. This will help you build your skills and become a more confident speaker and writer of English. Make sure that you understand the work in each unit before you go on to the next one. Remember to have a dictionary handy as you work through the book, and to ask for help if you need it. There is a glossary on pages 97–98 that explains the grammatical terms used in the units.

I hope you enjoy reading the texts and doing all the activities.

Good luck!

Laura Anderson

About this book

This book consists of sixteen units, each covering one or more aspects of grammar or punctuation. Each unit is theme-based and contains two texts designed to introduce the grammatical features and to show students how they function in context. These are followed by detailed explanations of how and why the grammar features are used, as well as exercises that allow students to put the knowledge they have acquired into practice. As an aid to revision, there is a glossary at the end of the book that summarises the grammatical terms used in the units.

The exercises in the units are organised as follows:

Let's find them!

- These exercises require students to find examples of the grammatical feature in question in the texts. They are straightforward exercises designed to test recall.

Let's go to the next step!

- This set of exercises is more difficult, requiring students to apply the knowledge they have acquired.

Let's aim high now!

- These are challenging exercises, again requiring students to apply what they have learnt.

Let's put it all together now!

- This is an editing exercise designed to test the students' understanding of the material covered in the whole unit. It also acts as a revision exercise.

Let's have fun!

- Although this exercise is designed to be fun, it is also challenging. It reinforces the material learnt.

Let's have a test!

- This series of eight NAPLAN-style questions helps students revise for the NAPLAN Tests and also tests their knowledge of the material learnt in the unit as a whole. The questions are graded so that the first two fall into Band 3, with each successive pair of questions moving into the next band.

Let's write now!

- This activity encourages students to write their own text in which they use the grammar and punctuation they have learnt in the unit. The texts are based on the theme and text types featured in the unit.

Most of the exercises in this book consist of seven questions, as we believe they give students the practice they need to fully grasp the rules of grammar and punctuation.

Unit 1 School excursions

Focus

Sentences: subjects and predicates

A visit to the bakery

Yesterday the Year 4s visited a bakery. A guide showed us around. We saw how the flour is mixed with yeast, salt, fat and water in a large mixing machine. Another machine divided the mixture into portions and then dropped them into pans. The pans were placed in a huge oven to bake for 25 minutes. The freshly baked loaves smelled delicious!

When the bread came out of the oven it was placed on racks to cool. A conveyor carried the loaves to the slicing machine. After that, they were packed and were ready to be delivered to shops and supermarkets.

The best part of our visit came right at the end. We each got a piece of dough. We kneaded, shaped, baked and ate it. Yum! It tasted amazing!

by Alexander

This is a **recount**. A recount tells about things that have already happened. Alexander uses **sentences** to tell about a visit to the bakery.

Sentences
- are groups of words that make sense when they stand on their own.
- are used to tell a story or anything else we want to write about.
- always start with a capital letter and end with a full stop, question mark or exclamation mark.

For example: **Yesterday the Year 4s visited a bakery.**

Let's find them!

Find the endings to these **sentence** beginnings in the text, and then fill them in. Remember to use the correct punctuation mark at the end of each sentence.

1. A guide showed ______
2. Another machine divided ______
3. The freshly baked loaves smelled ______
4. A conveyor carried ______
5. The best part of our visit came ______
6. We each got ______
7. It tasted ______

Let's go to the next step!

These **sentences** are missing capital letters and full stops. Can you write them correctly?

1. our next excursion will be to the Botanic Gardens
2. lots of schools were visiting the museum that day
3. we went on an excursion to the art gallery last term
4. our teachers arrange lots of excursions for us every year
5. one of my favourite places for a school excursion is the beach
6. a man at the museum gave us directions to the dinosaur exhibit
7. school excursions are fun for the students, but not always for the teachers

Let's aim high now!

These **sentences** don't make sense because some of the words are in the wrong place. Work out where the words should be and then write the **sentences** correctly; for example,

On an excursion to the zoo went our class. ×

Our class went on an excursion to the zoo. ✓

Don't forget to start each **sentence** with a capital letter!

1. Lots of interesting animals at the zoo saw we.
2. The zoo every year visit thousands of students.
3. More interesting than others are some excursions.
4. A recount about our visit to the zoo write we had to.
5. The children right in front of the museum dropped the bus.
6. Our lunch near the giraffes' enclosure ate my friends and I.
7. Us about the zoo's education program told the education officer.

From: Melissa Ho
Subject: Botanic Gardens
Date: 18 August
To: Sophie Wright sowright@firstnetwork.com.au

Hi Soph

I hope you're enjoying your holiday. When are you coming back to school?

I told Mr Fletcher that I was going to email you, and he said I must tell you about our excursion to the Botanic Gardens. **We went there today**. It was very interesting. An Aboriginal man showed us around the Cadi Jam Ora: First Encounters Garden. In the garden are indigenous plants and the kinds of plants the first white settlers tried to grow. Our guide told us that when the first Europeans came to Sydney in 1788, Aboriginal people called the Cadigal lived here. The plants the white settlers put in did not grow very well. The Cadigal caught diseases like smallpox from the white settlers and most of them died from these diseases. I think that's so sad.

I still have to write a recount about the excursion for homework, so I'd better go now.

See you soon.

Melissa

This is an **email**. An email is a way of communicating with others. Melissa uses **sentences** containing **subjects** and **predicates** to tell her friend about the class's excursion to the Botanic Gardens.

Sentences always contain a **verb**; for example, We **went** there today.

Simple sentences can be divided into two parts—the **subject**, that does the action, and the **predicate**, that tells what happens to the **subject** and contains the **verb**; for example, **We** is the subject and **went there today** is the predicate.

Let's find them!

Use verbs from the text to complete these **simple sentences**.

1. Today we ____________ on an excursion to the Botanic Gardens.
2. It ____________ very interesting.
3. An Aboriginal man ____________ us around the garden.
4. There ____________ indigenous plants in the garden.
5. The first Europeans ____________ to Sydney in 1788.
6. The Cadigal ____________ diseases like smallpox.
7. The Cadigal ____________ from these diseases.

Let's go to the next step!

Choose a **subject** from the box to complete each of these **sentences**.

The Year 6s	My worksheet	A large bird	Our teacher
The little boy	I	The bus driver	

1. ____________________ am looking forward to the music camp.
2. ____________________ blew away at the beach.
3. ____________________ ate my lunch at the zoo.
4. ____________________ drove past the theatre.
5. ____________________ counted us outside the museum.
6. ____________________ are going to Canberra next week.
7. ____________________ left his hat on a bench at the Botanic Gardens.

Let's aim high now!

Match the **subjects** in Column A with their **predicates** in Column B. Shade the matching pairs the same colour. The first one has been done for you.

Subjects	Predicates
1 Our class	took us to the wrong place.
2 The lady at the observatory	taught us about energy and movement.
3 The bus driver	have been on three excursions this year.
4 Our guide at the museum	let us look through a telescope.
5 The visit to the CSIRO	went on a tour of the art gallery.
6 The people at the CSIRO	has been my favourite excursion so far.
7 Those students	told us where the fossils were from.

Let's put it together now!

This student has forgotten the rules for writing **sentences**. Show him where the sentences are by filling in the capital letters and full stops with a red pen.

last week the Year 3s and 4s went to a studio an orchestra played music for us the conductor told us about the different instruments he asked us lots of questions one of my friends conducted the orchestra he did a good job the conductor congratulated him afterwards

Let's have fun!

Put together the **subjects** and **predicates** on these puzzle pieces to make five **sentences**. The pictures will help you put the right pieces together. Write the sentences in the spaces.

For example:

The children saw koalas at the wildlife centre.

Let's have a test!

Tip!
Shade the circle next to the correct answer.

1 Which group of words is a sentence?

- ○ our class to the aquarium to see the dugongs
- ○ our class to see the dugongs to the aquarium
- ○ Our class went to the aquarium to see the dugongs.
- ○ to the aquarium to see the dugongs

2 Which group of words is **not** a sentence?

- ○ The insects were in a glass cabinet.
- ○ in a glass cabinet at the museum
- ○ That is where we saw the insects.
- ○ The glass cabinet was in the museum.

3 Which sentence has been written correctly?

- ○ The play the whole class enjoyed.
- ○ The whole class the play enjoyed.
- ○ The whole class enjoyed the play.
- ○ The play enjoyed the whole class.

4 Which sentence has **not** been written correctly?

- ○ We saw amazing paintings at the art gallery.
- ○ There are amazing paintings at the art gallery.
- ○ The art gallery is full of amazing paintings.
- ○ We to the art gallery last week.

5 Which subject completes this sentence correctly?

____________________ swam around in huge tanks.

- ○ The aquarium
- ○ The fish
- ○ The spectators
- ○ The tour guide

6 Which subject does **not** complete this sentence correctly?

____________________ stepped onto the stage.

- ○ The actors
- ○ The curtains
- ○ The performers
- ○ The dancers

7 Which predicate completes this sentence correctly?

The cutest animals at the zoo ____________________

- ○ is a chimpanzee.
- ○ has the chimpanzees.
- ○ are the chimpanzees.
- ○ was the chimpanzees.

8 Which group of words does **not** complete this sentence correctly?

My teacher ____________________________________

- ○ likes taking us on excursions.
- ○ often us on excursions.
- ○ says she likes taking us on excursions.
- ○ often takes us on excursions.

Let's write now!

Write a **recount** about a school excursion you've been on. Remember to start your **sentences** with capital letters and to end them with full stops.

Unit 2 So that's how it works!

Focus
Sentences: statements, questions, exclamations and commands

Flying high!

In the centre of the bright halo was a silver disc. It hovered above the paddock for a minute or two, and then slowly descended. When it came to rest, it seemed to pull in the light around it, like a tortoise retreating into its shell. "**What is it?**" asked Jan. It looked like a wide-brimmed silver hat on legs.

"Whatever it is, I'd like to see what's inside it," said Billy.

"How are you going to do that?" asked Jan. "There's no way in."

"There must be a way," replied Billy, walking slowly around the craft.

Suddenly he stopped. "Look at this, Jan," he said.

"Have you found something?" she asked, coming to join him.

"I'm not sure. What do you think this is for?" he asked, as he placed his finger on what looked like a small dent. Immediately, part of the surface slid aside, creating an entry into the craft. "So that's how it works!" muttered Billy.

This is part of a **narrative**. A narrative tells a story. The author uses **statements** to give information and **questions** to show how the characters ask for information while telling about the strange craft that landed in Billy and Jan's paddock.

Statements and **questions** are types of sentences.
Statements are sentences that give information or opinions.
They always end with a full stop (.).
For example: **In the centre of the bright halo was a silver disc.**
Questions are sentences that ask for information.
They always end with a question mark (?).
For example: **"What is it?"**

Let's find them!

Complete these **statements** and **questions** from the text with their correct endings. Remember to use the correct punctuation mark at the end of each sentence.

1. It hovered above the paddock for a minute or two, ______________________
2. It looked like ______________________
3. Suddenly ______________________
4. Immediately, part of the surface slid aside, ______________________

5. How are ______________________________
6. Have you ______________________________
7. What do you think ______________________________

Let's go to the next step!

Fill in the correct **punctuation** mark at the end of each of these sentences.

1. He used a trolley to move that object
2. Which machine would you rather buy
3. Why do furniture removers use ramps
4. Do you know that a ramp is a useful tool
5. Some tools make a gardener's job easier
6. How many machines are there in his shed
7. I would dig the hole with that shovel over there

Let's aim high now!

Match the **question** in Column A with the **statement** that answers it in Column B. Shade the matching pairs the same colour.

Question	Statement
1 How do I unlock this door?	1 They are carried in large trucks.
2 What sets a bicycle in motion?	2 You could try turning the key.
3 How can I turn this water into ice?	3 You can use my hammer.
4 What is the purpose of a machine?	4 Yes, he has a ladder.
5 Will he be able to get onto the roof?	5 I suggest you put it in the freezer.
6 Can you help me get this nail into the wood?	6 It makes work easier.
7 How are goods transported around the country?	7 It'll move if someone pushes or pedals it.

Flying high! (Part two)

Just as Billy was wondering how they were going to get into the craft, a stairway appeared before them.

"**How cool is that!**" said Billy, and immediately started up the steps.

"Be careful," Jan called after him, but Billy was already inside the craft.

"Wow! Would you look at this, Jan!" he exclaimed, beckoning to his sister.

Jan quickly mounted the steps. Inside everything glowed with a soft, multi-coloured light.

"This is unbelievable!" gasped Jan.

A booming voice from somewhere in the craft made the children jump. "**Sit down**. Drink this." Two chairs and a tray containing two glasses of a bright green liquid slid towards them. The children did as they were told. The drink was delicious! "Put the glasses on the tray." Again the twins did as they were told and the tray slid back into the wall. Billy finally found his voice. "How do you do that?" he asked.

The voice answered, "Get up. Come with me. I will show you how it works."

This is another part of the **narrative**. The author uses **exclamations** to show how the characters express emotions and **commands** to show how they give instructions.

Exclamations

- are sentences that express strong emotions, or feelings.
- always end with an exclamation mark (!); for example, **How cool is that!**

Commands

- are sentences that tell someone to do something, or give an order.
- start with a verb, or action word.
- end with a full stop or exclamation mark; for example, **Sit down.**

Let's find them!

Find these sentences in the text, and then write down whether they are **exclamations** or **commands**.

1. Would you look at this, Jan! ____________________
2. This is unbelievable! ____________________
3. Drink this. ____________________
4. The drink was delicious! ____________________
5. Put the glasses on the tray. ____________________
6. Get up. ____________________
7. Come with me. ____________________

Let's go to the next step!

Complete each sentence with a **full stop** or an **exclamation mark**.

1. Use scissors ____________________
2. Undo the clasps ____________________
3. What a brilliant invention ____________________
4. Put the wheels on the cart ____________________
5. How amazing is that machine ____________________
6. I can't believe my invention works ____________________
7. Show your sister how to tie her shoelaces ____________________

Let's aim high now!

Tip!
Reminder! Each word starts with a capital letter because it comes at the beginning of the sentence.

Choose a word from the box to start each **exclamation** or **command**. Use each word once only.

place	attach	what	push	this	how	slip

1. ____________________ a fantastic tool this is!
2. ____________________ the trolley and it will start moving.
3. ____________________ is the best scooter that was ever invented!
4. ____________________ amazing that such a large machine can fly!
5. ____________________ a handle to the brush to turn it into a broom.
6. ____________________ a wedge under the door to stop it from slamming.
7. ____________________ the rope around the wheel and then see if your pulley works.

Let's put it together now!

This student has used the wrong punctuation marks at the end of some of her **sentences**. Use a red pen to make the corrections.

"How does it work. There must be some way to get it started," said Matt. Chen flicked the switch on and off again? This time it did work. The little red car sped across the room and crashed into the wall. The boys looked at each other! "That was awesome?" exclaimed Rob. "Link it up to the computer, Matt, and let's try to control it this time. Do you need the instructions."

Matt shook his head. He'd gone over it so many times in his head, he knew exactly what to do? "We've done it, guys?" exclaimed Chen. "We've finally done it!"

Let's have fun!

Make the monkey laugh!

Find out how to make the monkey laugh by decoding the **question**, **command**, **statement** and **exclamation** below. The key that will help you unlock the monkey's secret is on the old scroll.

A = △	J = ✎	S = ✻
B = ☪	K = ✋	T = ♣
C = ❖	L = ⭘	U = ▮
D = ⌘	M = ⊙	V = ☮
E = ✜	N = &	W = ❮
F = ✚	O = ▯	X = ℵ
G = +	P = ▲	Y = ♠
H = ◗	Q = ➘	Z = ⊇
I = ◈	R = ◁	

1. ❮▯▮⭘⌘ ♠▯▮ ⭘◈✋✜ ♣▯ ✋&▯❮ ⊙♠ ✻✜❖◁✜♣?

2. ♣◈❖✋⭘✜ △ ▲△◁♣ ▯✚ ⊙♠ ☪▯⌘♠.

3. ◈♣'✻ ✜◈♣◗✜◁ ⊙♠ ❖◗◈&, ▯◁ ♣◗✜ ♣◗✜▲ ▯✚ ⊙♠ &▯✻✜.

4. ◈♣'✻ ◗◈✻ ❖◗◈&!

So how do you make the monkey laugh? Write your answer as a command.

Let's have a test!

1 Which sentence is a statement?

- ◯ Is this a pulley?
- ◯ What a great pulley!
- ◯ This is a pulley.
- ◯ Use the pulley.

2 Which sentence is **not** a statement?

- ◯ My mother uses a rolling pin.
- ◯ Place the rolling pin on the table.
- ◯ My mother bought a new rolling pin.
- ◯ A rolling pin is a handy tool.

3 Which punctuation mark completes this sentence correctly?

What kind of simple tool is a rake

◯ !   ◯ .   ◯ ?   ◯ ,

4 Which sentence has **not** been punctuated correctly?

- ◯ Do you know how your new computer works!
- ◯ Switch on your new computer.
- ◯ I have learnt how to use my new computer.
- ◯ I love my new computer!

5 Which sentence is a command?

- ◯ The stapler needs more staples.
- ◯ Put more staples in the stapler.
- ◯ What a smart new stapler you have!
- ◯ Have you put more staples in the stapler?

6 Which word completes this command correctly?

__________________ the plug into the socket and then switch on the fan.

◯ Insert   ◯ Attach   ◯ Pull   ◯ Connect

7 Which punctuation mark completes this sentence correctly?

How cool is Jason's robot __________________

◯ .   ◯ !   ◯ ?   ◯ ,

8 Which sentence has been punctuated correctly?

- ◯ Is that how it works!
- ◯ I'll show you how it works!
- ◯ So that's how it works!
- ◯ Show me how it works!

Let's write now!

What happened to Billy and Jan? Who, or what, was the voice? What was behind the wall?

Continue the **narrative** by writing two more paragraphs and a conclusion. Although you will use mainly **statements** in your narrative, try using some **questions**, **exclamations** and **commands** as well.

Unit 3 Endangered animals

Focus
Common nouns; proper nouns—capital letters

Numbats

Numbats are small, pouchless marsupials. **Conservationists** are trying to protect them. Today we mainly see **numbats** in **zoos**. They look a bit like squirrels. They have reddish brown **coats**, with six or seven white stripes across the back. They measure 35 to 45 cm from the tip of their pointed snouts to the end of their long, bushy tails.

Numbats feed mainly on termites. They catch the termites with their long, sticky tongues.

When the first white settlers arrived in the country more than two hundred years ago, numbats were quite common. Since then, numbat numbers have decreased because of the loss of their habitat and the introduction of foxes, domestic cats and dogs.

by Nina

This is an **information report**. An information report provides information and facts. Nina uses **common nouns** to name general people, animals, places and things in her report about numbats.

Common nouns are the general names of people, animals, places and things. For example: **conservationists**, **numbats**, **zoos**, **coats**.

Let's find them!

Find these **common nouns** in the text.

1. the animals numbats look like ____________________
2. the marks across the numbat's back ____________________
3. the insects that numbats feed on ____________________
4. the things numbats use to catch their food ____________________
5. the people who came to live in the country long ago ____________________
6. wild animals that became a threat to the numbat ____________________
7. domesticated animals that became a threat to the numbat ____________________

Let's go to the next step!

Underline the **common nouns** in these **sentences**; for example, Some snakes that live in the desert are endangered.

1. This rare parrot is an endangered bird.
2. We saw two big pandas when we went to the zoo.
3. Some elephants in certain countries are endangered.
4. There are many reptiles on the list of endangered animals.
5. This particular possum has large front teeth for cracking nuts.
6. Turtles that live in swamps feed on tadpoles, shrimps and worms.
7. Many endangered marsupials feed on the gum and sap of eucalyptus trees.

Let's aim high now!

Complete each **sentence** with a **common noun** from the box. The word in brackets will help you choose the correct noun.

tigers	tag	penguin	scientist
cave	students	ocean	

1. Inside the ____________________ we saw bats hanging upside down. (place)
2. I tried to rescue the little ____________________ from the oily water. (animal)
3. I watched the man inject a ____________________ under the animal's skin. (thing)
4. Many of the world's endangered animals live in the ____________________. (place)
5. ____________________ are beautiful mammals with black stripes on their coats. (animal)
6. I spoke to a ____________________ who studies the behaviour of dolphins. (person)
7. The ____________________ at our school think we should try to save endangered animals. (people)

Dugongs

Dugongs are large, grey marine mammals. They live in the **Indian Ocean** and Pacific Ocean between Africa and the islands of Vanuatu. The world's biggest dugong population lives in Shark Bay off the coast of Western Australia.

Dugongs can grow up to three metres in length and weigh up to 400 kilograms. Their diet consists of sea grass, which grows on the ocean floor in warm, shallow waters.

Female dugongs give birth to a single calf every three to seven years. The calves are born between **August** and December. The calf stays close to its mother and drinks milk from her teats for the first one or two years of its life. When danger threatens, the young dugong hides behind its mother.

Threats to the dugong include sharks, saltwater crocodiles, killer whales and humans.

Dugongs are a protected species in Australia.

by Brad

This is another **information report**. Brad uses **proper nouns** to name particular places and times in his report about dugongs.

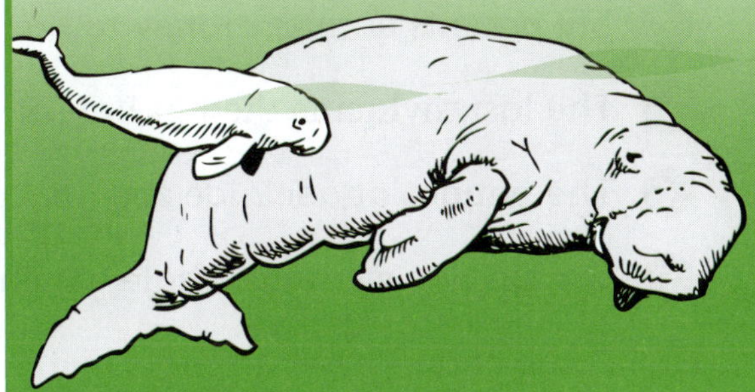

Proper nouns
- are the particular names of people, animals, places or things; for example, **Indian Ocean**.
- include the names of the days of the week and the months of the year; for example, **August**.
- always start with a **capital letter**.

Rule! If the particular name of a person, animal, place or thing has more than one word in it, all of the words start with a **capital letter**; for example, **Indian Ocean**.

Let's find them!

Find these **proper nouns** in the text.

1. the person who wrote the report about dugongs ______
2. a continent ______
3. a group of islands ______
4. the place where a large population of dugongs lives ______

5. the state in the west of Australia ______________________________

6. the last month of the year ______________________________

7. the country where dugongs are protected ______________________________

Let's go to the next step!

Underline the **proper nouns** in these sentences and give them capital letters; for example, I took my friend Jack to see the dugongs at Mermaid Lagoon.

1. My dog waggles is not an endangered animal!
2. My parents donate money to the world wildlife fund.
3. The last thylacine died in hobart zoo in september 1936.
4. The pandas at adelaide zoo are called wang wang and funi.
5. On tuesday we went whale watching in a boat called sandpiper.
6. Some endangered animals live in the blue mountains in new south wales.
7. A type of frog that lives near the murray river could become extinct one day.

Let's aim high now!

Complete each sentence with a **proper noun** from the box.

Miss Swann	Colo	Mr Stevens	July
Melbourne Zoo	England	Wildlife Conservation Society	

1. There are no longer any wild wolves in ______________________.
2. The first gorilla born in captivity was called ______________________.
3. Next year in ______________________ we are going to visit the new marine park.
4. The conservationist was a man called ______________________.
5. Our teacher, ______________________, showed us pictures of endangered animals.
6. Zoos like ______________________ are trying to save endangered animals.
7. The ______________________ works to save endangered animals.

Let's put it together now!

This student has written seven **common** and **proper** nouns incorrectly in this part of his report. Use a red pen to underline the mistakes and make the corrections.

This little Lizard is found in the Mount lofty Ranges near adelaide in South Australia. There are fewer than 6000 of these little reptiles left in australia. The main reason they are dying out is that their Habitat is being destroyed. The lizards find safety in spider Holes, so in areas where there are more spider holes, there are more of these little Reptiles.

Let's have fun!

The clues will help you complete this crossword puzzle. The answers are all **common** or **proper nouns**, and most of them can be found in the texts in this unit.

Across

1. a large, grey marine mammal
4. the last month of the year
6. the name of an ocean
7. These endangered marsupials have long, bushy ones.
8. the name of a bay off the coast of Western Australia
10. This substance is found in the sea.
11. the opposite of brother

Down

2. an endangered marsupial
3. a large continent
5. domesticated felines
7. Numbats eat these insects.
9. another name for people

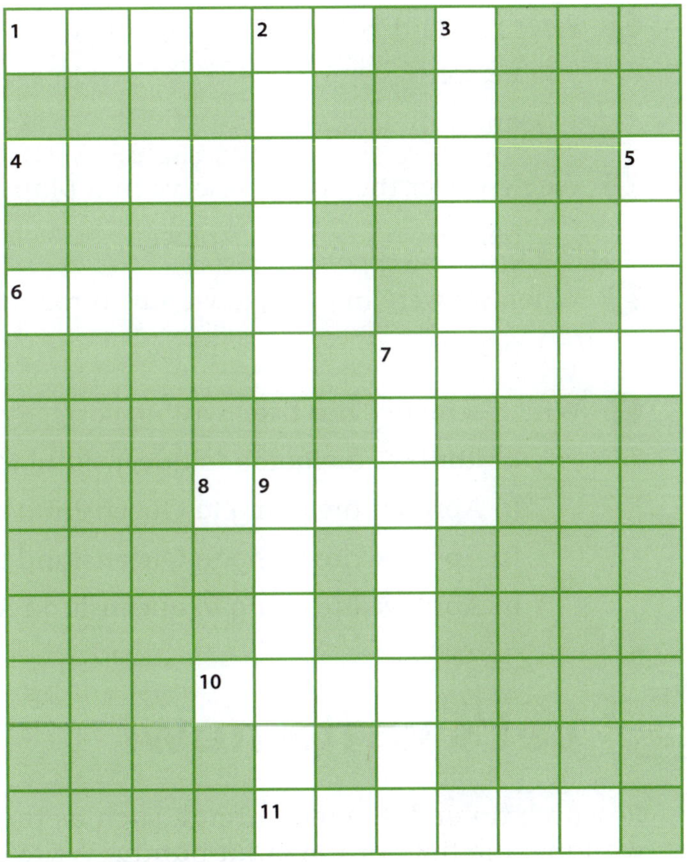

Let's have a test!

In questions 1–3, show whether the underlined word is the name of a person, place, animal or thing.

1. There are very few wild gorillas left in the world.
   - ◯ person ◯ place ◯ animal ◯ thing
2. Wild gorillas live in forests in Africa.
   - ◯ person ◯ place ◯ animal ◯ thing
3. The ranger told us where we could see the spotted marsh frog.
   - ◯ person ◯ place ◯ animal ◯ thing
4. Which sentence has been written correctly?
   - ◯ We saw lots of endangered Birds at the bird park.
   - ◯ We saw lots of endangered Birds at the bird Park.
   - ◯ We saw lots of endangered birds at the Bird park.
   - ◯ We saw lots of endangered birds at the bird park.

In questions 5–7, show whether the underlined word is the name of a person, place, animal or thing.

5. Peter Herman is writing a book about the blue whale.
   - ◯ person ◯ place
   - ◯ animal ◯ thing
6. We flew over the nature reserve in a plane called Bluebird.
   - ◯ person ◯ place ◯ animal ◯ thing
7. When we were in Canada we saw a rare leatherback turtle.
   - ◯ person ◯ place ◯ animal ◯ thing
8. Which sentence has been written correctly?
   - ◯ In april we are going to queensland to see a rare reptile.
   - ◯ In April we are going to Queensland to see a rare Reptile.
   - ◯ In April we are going to Queensland to see a rare reptile.
   - ◯ In April we are going to queensland to see a rare reptile.

Let's write now!

Research an endangered animal, such as the Tasmanian devil, the brush-tailed rock wallaby, the tiger or the giant panda. Write an **information report** about the animal you have chosen. Use **common** and **proper nouns** to name people, animals, places and things.

Unit 4 Tales from long ago

Focus

Collective nouns, compound nouns and abstract nouns

A folktale from Africa

It was time for King Leopard to choose his successor. He sent out a message to all the animals in the kingdom, telling them to meet at his palace.

From sunrise to sunset, hordes of animals could be seen making their way to the palace. When everyone was assembled, Leopard looked down at his **audience** and told them that the one who could throw a spear into the sky and count to ten before it landed would be the next king.

A hyena stepped out of the pack and took the spear. It landed before he got to three. Then a baboon from a noisy troop stepped forward. He managed to get to four. Many other animals tried, from tiny **earthworms** and fireflies to huge hippos and elephants, but none was successful. Finally a little antelope from a small herd took the spear. He jumped as high as he could, threw the spear skywards and quickly counted, "Five plus five is ten!"

Leopard chose the antelope as his successor because he was the cleverest of all the animals.

This is a **folktale**. A folktale is a type of **narrative**. The author uses **collective** nouns to name groups of animals and **compound nouns** to name other animals and things in nature while telling how Leopard chose his successor.

Collective nouns are the names of groups of people, animals, places and things; for example, **audience**.

Compound nouns are the names of people, animals, places and things that are formed by joining two or more words together; for example, **earthworms** is formed by joining the words **earth** and **worms**.

Tip! Some compound nouns are written as hyphenated words or two words; for example, **mother-in-law, bus stop.**

Let's find them!

Find these **collective** and **compound nouns** in the text.

1. groups of animals ______________________
2. a group of hyenas ______________________

3. a group of baboons ____________________

4. a group of antelope ____________________

5. the time when the sun comes up ____________________

6. the time when the sun goes down ____________________

7. insects that glow in the dark ____________________

Let's go to the next step!

Circle the **collective nouns** and underline the **compound nouns** in these sentences; for example, There is a book of folktales in the library.

1. Jody is the best storyteller in our class.
2. My grandmother told me a tale about a gang of thieves.
3. In the story, a plague of locusts invades the countryside.
4. Today we read a story about a woodcutter who lived in a forest.
5. This tale is about a colony of bats that turns into humans at daybreak.
6. I listened to the collection of stories while sitting in my favourite armchair.
7. The scariest story in the book is about a criminal mastermind who has his own army.

Let's aim high now!

Write these words from folktales under the correct headings.

full moon	son-in-law	heap	cluster	batch
crowd	bouquet	chopsticks	tribe	rainbow
fairy tale	housework	toadstool	litter	

Collective nouns	Compound nouns

A Japanese folktale

Hidesato loved the peacefulness and coolness of the forest. His favourite spot was a small clearing beside a stream, where he would sit and watch the water rippling by. One day, when he came to the little bridge that crossed the stream, he found a large serpent blocking his path. Hidesato felt no fear and calmly stepped over it. The serpent immediately changed into a woman of great **beauty**. She congratulated Hidesato on his bravery and asked him to destroy a huge centipede that had killed her sons. Hidesato felt the woman's **sorrow** and agreed to help her.

That night, as he kept watch on the bridge, Hidesato saw two green eyes emerging from the darkness. Their brightness almost blinded him, but he managed to shoot off two arrows. Both arrows hit their mark, and the centipede lay dead.

For the first time in many years, the woman knew happiness. She rewarded Hidesato with many gifts.

This is another **folktale**. The author uses **abstract nouns** to name qualities, states of being and feelings while telling of Hidesato's adventure.

Abstract nouns are the names of abstract ideas, such as qualities, feelings and states of being; for example, **beauty**, **sorrow**.

Let's find them!

Tip!

We cannot see or touch abstract nouns. Many of them end with the suffix **-ness**; for example, **kindness**.

Find these **abstract nouns** in the text.

1. the state of being peaceful ____________________
2. the state of being cool ____________________
3. the feeling of being frightened ____________________
4. the state of being brave ____________________
5. the state of being dark ____________________
6. the state of being bright ____________________
7. the feeling of being happy ____________________

Let's go to the next step!

Underline the **abstract nouns** in these sentences; for example, Many folktales are about friendship.

1. The prince was dazzled by the brilliance of her smile.
2. In the story, the people were punished for their greed.
3. The prince showed great courage in overcoming the dragon.
4. Many stories teach us the importance of being kind to others.
5. The wizard's wickedness was well known throughout the land.
6. The children were filled with wonder when they heard the story.
7. The story is about a poor man who is rewarded for his generosity.

Let's aim high now!

Tip! Psst! All of the sentence beginnings contain abstract nouns.

Complete these sentences from famous folktales by matching the sentence beginnings with their endings. Shade the matching pairs the same colour. The first one has been done for you.

Sentence beginnings	Sentence endings
1 In a fit of rage,	1 the queen watched her son receive his prize.
2 Showing great loyalty,	2 the king announced that the next day would be a holiday.
3 Using his imagination,	3 the wicked queen smashed the mirror into thousands of pieces.
4 With a feeling of pride,	4 the two girls gave each other a special gift.
5 In a moment of uncertainty,	5 the king's servants remained with him.
6 With a burst of speed,	6 the prince looked to his father for guidance.
7 To celebrate their victory,	7 the inventor made two pairs of wings.
8 As a mark of their friendship,	8 the hare raced towards the finishing line.

Let's put it together now!

This student has left out the following **nouns** in her story. Can you fill them in for her?

sadness	flock	family	marketplace
greed	snowfall	horror	

A folktale from India

A swan with golden feathers once tried to help a poor ____________. It gave them one feather a day to sell at the ____________. But then the mother was filled with ____________. She told her children to help her pluck all the swan's feathers. As they held the golden feathers, they watched in ____________ as they turned into chicken feathers! The swan was filled with ____________ and hid amongst the reeds. Before the first ____________, she joined another ____________ and flew away.

Let's have fun!

1. Making up **collective nouns** is a lot of fun. Which words from the box could be used to describe these groups? Write them beneath the pictures; for example:

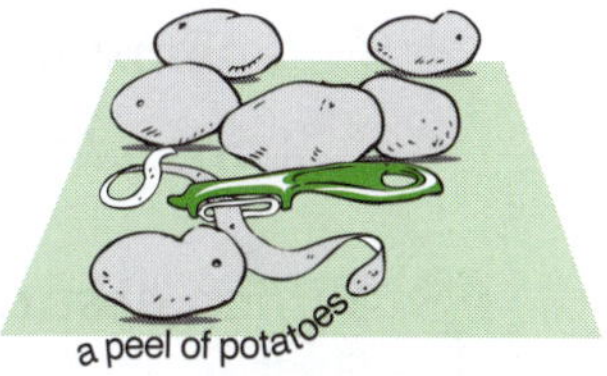

peel	howl
slice	flame

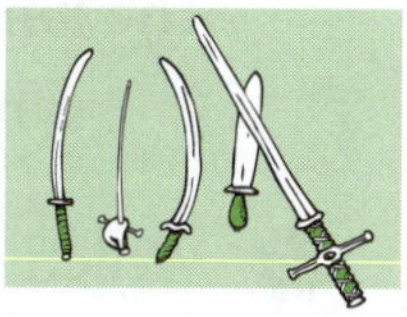

____________ ____________ ____________

2. Find these **compound nouns** from a popular folktale in the wordsearch puzzle. The words go forwards, backwards, up and down.

grandmother	silkworm	heartbeat
housework	downpour	

t	a	e	b	t	r	a	e	h	c	z	r
t	u	x	p	k	b	x	d	a	h	m	e
w	h	o	u	s	e	w	o	r	k	n	h
s	t	y	w	f	n	m	z	e	f	g	t
c	v	g	a	h	m	f	w	q	d	h	o
n	d	q	m	o	l	f	x	z	o	u	m
m	r	o	w	k	l	i	s	h	w	k	d
c	u	g	h	j	s	y	j	s	n	s	n
b	f	g	s	h	a	f	h	c	p	a	a
w	c	h	o	m	q	g	w	j	o	p	r
z	d	w	j	k	s	u	n	l	u	d	g
y	h	y	h	s	h	e	t	n	r	m	w

3. Use lines to match an **abstract noun** to each sentence. The first one has been done for you.

That's better!	shock
How frightening!	fun
Well done!	improvement
I don't believe it!	obedience
Thank goodness that's over!	fear
Thank you so much!	relief
I'm enjoying this!	gratitude
I always do as I'm told.	congratulations

Let's have a test!

Which collective nouns complete these sentences correctly?

1. An ____________ of soldiers approached the village.
   - ◯ crew ◯ horde ◯ army ◯ pack

2. The poor woodcutter had only one ____________ of firewood left.
   - ◯ string ◯ bundle ◯ library ◯ forest

3. Which sentence contains a compound noun?
   - ◯ When the princess cried, her teardrops turned into diamonds.
   - ◯ The poor family lived in a little cottage.
   - ◯ My friend gave me a book of exciting stories for Christmas.
   - ◯ They are making my favourite story into a movie.

4. Which of these words is **not** a compound noun?
   - ◯ gemstones ◯ cupcakes
   - ◯ monsters ◯ grandfather

5. Which abstract noun completes this sentence correctly?

   The knight fought with great ____________ during the fierce battle.
   - ◯ sympathy ◯ courage ◯ disgust ◯ surprise

6. Which abstract noun does **not** complete this sentence correctly?

   The king ruled his people with great ____________.
   - ◯ kindness ◯ skill ◯ wisdom ◯ opportunity

7. Which sentence contains an abstract noun?
   - ◯ This folktale has a lot of humour in it. ◯ This folktale is very long.
   - ◯ This folktale is very interesting. ◯ This folktale is very funny.

8. Which sentence does **not** contain an abstract noun?
   - ◯ The kind man was rewarded with great wealth.
   - ◯ The kind man was always prepared to help others.
   - ◯ The kind man received his reward with pride.
   - ◯ The kind man was rewarded for his helpfulness.

Let's write now!

Choose a folktale you know and retell it in your own words. Try to use at least one **collective noun**, one **compound noun** and one **abstract noun** in your **narrative**. If you can use more than one of these nouns, that would be great!

Unit 5 Pirates

Focus
Plural nouns

http://www.pirategames.com.au

HOME | PIRATES! | PIRATE ADVENTURES | PIRATE GAMES | FAMOUS PIRATES

Edward Teach (Blackbeard)

To some people, **pirates** were heroes, but to others, they were **villains**. One of the most famous pirates was Edward Teach, or Blackbeard, as he was known. Three hundred years ago, he and his crew sailed around the Caribbean looking for ships to plunder. Brandishing swords, **cutlasses** and pistols, they struck terror into the hearts of sailors. They ransacked ships' **cargoes**, taking treasure such as coins, emeralds, topazes and valuable dishes, as well as food and weapons. According to eyewitness accounts, Teach made himself look more fearsome by putting lighted matches into his long beard. When he was fighting, there was always a cloud of smoke around his head.

This is a **website**. One of the purposes of a website is to provide information. The author uses **plural nouns** to name people and things in this website article about a famous pirate.

Plural nouns

- are the names of more than one person, animal, place or thing; for example, **pirates**.

Rule!

- For most nouns, add *s* to make them plural ; for example **villain → villains**.
- For nouns that end in *s*, *x*, *z*, *sh* or *ch*, add *es*; for example, **cutlass → cutlasses**, **mix → mixes**, **buzz → buzzes**, **lash → lashes**, **latch → latches**.
- For some nouns that end in *o* and that have a consonant before the *o*, add *es*; for example, **cargo → cargoes**.

Let's find them!

Tip!
If a noun ends in *o* and there is a vowel before the *o*, add *s* to make it plural; for example, **radio → radios**.

Find these **plural nouns** in the text.

Write the plural of

1. hero ______
2. ship ______
3. pistol ______
4. topaz ______
5. dish ______

6. weapon ______________________________

7. match ______________________________

Let's go to the next step!

Write the **plurals** of these words from pirate stories; for example, **dagger → daggers**.

Singular	Plural	Singular	Plural
galleon		rope	
mast		rash	
sash		tax	
cross		beach	
catch		potato	
moustache		mosquito	
crash		cameo	

Let's aim high now!

Write the words in brackets as **plural nouns**.

1. The sailor hid from the pirates in the (rush) ______________________.
2. The sailor grabbed two (bunch) ______________________ of grapes.
3. The pirate and his crew sailed the seven (sea) ______________________.
4. The pirates' (chest) ______________________ were full of stolen treasure.
5. The fur on the pirate's cloak comes from two (fox) ______________________.
6. The pirates found (calico) ______________________ and silks amongst the ship's cargo.
7. The pirate ship has been battered by two (tornado) ______________________ this year.

http://www.pirategames.com.au

HOME | PIRATES! | PIRATE ADVENTURES | PIRATE GAMES | FAMOUS PIRATES

Female pirates

There are lots of **stories** about pirates. There are even stories about women who became pirates, like Anne Bonny and Mary Read. They certainly didn't act like ladies! They disguised themselves as men by wearing trousers and jackets and tying scarves around their heads. They armed themselves with **knives**, swords and pistols, and could fight as well as any of the **men**. The stories tell us that they spent exciting lives plundering ships and collecting treasures such as **gold**, silver, diamonds and rubies.

This is another article from a **website**. The author uses **plural nouns** to name people and things while telling about female pirates.

Here are some more rules for writing **plural nouns**.

Rule!

- For nouns that end in *y* and that have a consonant before the *y*, change the *y* to *i* and add *es*; for example, **story → stories**.
- For some nouns that end in *f* or *fe*, change the *f* to *v* and add *es*; for example, **knife → knives**.
- Some plural nouns are formed by changing the vowels and/or the endings; for example, **man → men**.
- Some words are always plural; for example, **gold**.

Let's find them!

Tip!

To turn these **nouns** that end in *f* into **plurals**, just add *s*: **reef → reefs**, **roof → roofs**, **chief → chiefs**, **cliff → cliffs**.

Find these **plural nouns** in the text.

Write the plural of

1. woman ____________________
2. lady ____________________
3. scarf ____________________
4. life ____________________
5. trousers ____________________
6. silver ____________________
7. ruby ____________________

Let's go to the next step!

Fill in the **plurals** of these nouns from pirate stories; for example, **beauty → beauties**.

Singular	Plural	Singular	Plural
duty		self	
sky		reef	
country		half	
army		dwarf	
party		measles	
spy		child	
cry		equipment	

Let's aim high now!

Complete each sentence with a **noun** from the box. Write the noun in its **plural** form. The first one has been done for you.

furniture	thief	baby	cliff
bully	shelf	seaman	bread

1. People who work on ships are called <u>seamen</u>.
2. The sailors ate ______________________ twice a day.
3. People who steal things are ______________________.
4. The pirates stole the flour that was on the ______________________.
5. People like pirates who hurt others are ______________________.
6. There usually aren't any little ______________________ on pirate ships.
7. The pirate ship anchored beneath some steep ______________________.
8. Some pirates boarded our ship and stole valuable ______________________.

Let's put it together now!

Can you find the seven **plural nouns** that this student has written incorrectly in his **article** on pirates? Circle them and write them out correctly in the spaces.

Problems for pirates

A pirate's life wasn't easy. If they received bad injurys to their arms or legs, the ship's carpenter would chop the limb off! Seamen also caught terrible diseases from all the rats, mouses and cockroachs on board. The type of work the seamen performed was also very dangerous. Another problem was not getting enough Vitamin C. There were no fridges in those days, so they couldn't keep fresh food like tomatos and oranges on board. To make sure they had enough fresh meat, they sometimes kept animales like chickens, calfs and even sheeps on board.

Let's have fun!

Find these objects on the pirate treasure map, and then write their names next to them. Make sure you write them in their **plural** form. One of them has been done for you.

- skull
- tree
- axe
- mango
- butterfly
- wolf
- goose
- salmon

Let's have a test!

In which sentences have the plural nouns been written **incorrectly**?

1
- ◯ Pirates used guns called muskets.
- ◯ Pirates stored their food in barreles.
- ◯ Pirates were sometimes called sea dogs.
- ◯ Pirates often stole food from other vessels.

2
- ◯ The pirate kept his treasure in boxes.
- ◯ The pirate was given twenty lashes.
- ◯ The injured pirate had to use crutchs.
- ◯ The pirate crew suffered many losses.

3
- ◯ In the days of the pirates, there were no radioes.
- ◯ The pirates listened to the echoes in the caves.
- ◯ The pirate ship sailed past two volcanoes.
- ◯ The pirates thought they were superheroes.

4
- ◯ The pirate had two canarys.
- ◯ The pirates kept away from big cities.
- ◯ The pirates' supplies were running low.
- ◯ The pirate's meat was covered in flies.

5
- ◯ Some pirates had wifes.
- ◯ The ship's deck was covered in leaves.
- ◯ The pirates were as vicious as wolves.
- ◯ The pirates wore kerchiefs around their heads.

6
- ◯ Many pirates lost their teeth.
- ◯ The pirate's hair was full of lice.
- ◯ Some pirates were excellent craftsmen.
- ◯ Some pirates had bare foots.

7 In which list has a plural noun been written **incorrectly**?
- ◯ cows, cattle and herds
- ◯ treasures, caskets and locks
- ◯ grandfathers, grandmothers and grandchilds
- ◯ scratches, spies and hooves

8 Which sequence of plurals completes this sentence correctly?

The pirate wore ____________, ____________ and ____________.
- ◯ bandanas, eye patchs, hats
- ◯ bandanas, eye patches, hats
- ◯ bandanaes, eye patches, hats
- ◯ bandanas, eye patches, hates

Let's write now!

Imagine your class is creating a **website** about pirates. Find out what you can about famous pirates, the way pirates dressed or anything else about pirates that you find interesting. Write an **article** for your website on the topic that you have chosen. Use **plural nouns** to name the people, animals, places or things that you write about.

Unit 6 Healthy living

Focus

Pronouns

BE WISE. EXERCISE

Plato's favourite pastimes are watching TV and playing computer games. **He** doesn't get much exercise. He isn't helping **himself**.

Emily's favourite pastimes are walking the dog, bike riding and playing basketball. She gets lots of exercise. She is helping herself.

Children who get plenty of exercise develop stronger muscles and bones. They also sleep better and cope better at school. Emily is one of them. Plato isn't.

Couch Potato Plato

Would you rather be like him

or like her?

Busy Bee Emily

If you'd rather be a busy bee, get off the couch and start buzzing about!

Visit us at <u>www.bwisexercise.com.au</u> and find out for yourself how you can become fitter, healthier and happier.

This is an **advertisement**. An advertisement persuades people to buy or do things. This advertisement has lots of **personal pronouns** in place of **common** and **proper nouns** to save repeating the nouns all the time.

Personal pronouns

- are used in place of nouns so that we don't have to repeat the names of people and things too much; for example, **He** is used in place of **Plato**.
- can refer back to a common or proper noun or another pronoun; for example, **himself** refers back to **Plato**.
- can be singular or plural.

Singular	Plural
I, me, myself	we, us, ourselves
you, yourself	you, yourselves
he, him, she, her, it, himself, herself, itself	they, them, themselves

Let's find them!

Find seven pronouns in the text and write them in the spaces. Use the list of singular and plural **personal pronouns** to help you find the words in the text.

1 ____________________

2 ____________________

Tip!

Personal pronouns that end in **self** or **selves** are also called **reflexive pronouns**. Some common mistakes that people make when using reflexive pronouns is to write **hisself** instead of **himself**, and **theirselves** instead of **themselves**. Look carefully at the reflexive pronouns in the list and make sure that you ALWAYS write them correctly!

3 ______________________

4 ______________________

5 ______________________

6 ______________________

7 ______________________

Let's go to the next step!

Complete these sentences with a **reflexive pronoun** from the box.

myself	ourselves	yourself	yourselves	herself	himself	themselves

1. She helped ______________ to some more salad.
2. They found ______________ in a group of runners.
3. "Make ______________ a health drink," Mum told Suzy.
4. He forced ______________ to continue doing the exercises.
5. We convinced ______________ that we could complete the course.
6. I watched ______________ in the mirror as I practised my tai chi moves.
7. "You can give ______________ a pat on the back," the coach said to the players.

Let's aim high now!

Which of these nouns do the **pronouns** in bold refer to? Use each option once. The first one has been done for you.

Ginny	the children	Jack	Veronica
The mother	the child	Julie and Jake	Advertisements

1. Sam gave **him** an apple at lunch time. Jack
2. Pass the ball to Ginny and **she** will score. ______________
3. **They** often encourage us to eat junk food. ______________
4. **She** put a banana in her daughter's lunch box. ______________
5. Julie and Jake made their lunches **themselves**. ______________
6. What have **you** got on your sandwich, Veronica? ______________
7. The child decided to try the healthy snack for **herself**. ______________
8. The teachers told **them** to get their PE equipment from their bags. ______________

PUT THE EAT BACK INTO HEALTHY.

Question: Whose lunch is healthier?

*What does **Felix** have in **his** lunchbox?*

What does Tania have in her lunch box?

Answer: His lunch is healthier than hers.

"Research has shown that children who eat a healthy diet develop stronger muscles, bones and teeth and their general health is better. That's why I make sure that my children take a healthy lunch to school. Are you doing the same for yours?"

Visit our website to find out how you can add a dose of health to your child's lunch box.
www.eatforhealth.com.au

This is another **advertisement**. It contains **possessive pronouns** instead of common and proper nouns to save repeating the nouns all the time, and **interrogative pronouns** to ask questions.

Possessive pronouns

- are used in place of common and proper nouns; for example, **his** in place of the boy's name.
- show ownership, or possession; for example, **his** shows that the lunch belongs to **him**.
- can be singular or plural.

Singular	Plural
my, mine	our, ours
your, yours	your, yours
his, her, hers, its	their, theirs

Interrogative pronouns ask questions; for example, **What?**

Let's find them!

Find seven **possessive** and **interrogative pronouns** in the text and write them in the spaces.

1 ______________________

2 ______________________

3 ______________________

4 ______________________

5 ______________________

Tip! The interrogative pronouns are **who, whom, whose, which** and **what**.

6 ______________________________

7 ______________________________

Let's go to the next step!

Choose the noun in the box that each **pronoun** in bold refers to. Use each option once. The first one has been done for you.

Uncle Joe	Lauren	Zack	apple
Jordan	Ken and Kathy	the dog	Mia and Casey

1. This skipping rope is **hers**. Lauren
2. I gave the dog **its** healthy treat this morning. ______________
3. "Look at **his** new exercise machine," said Dad. ______________
4. "This soccer ball is **yours**," the coach told Zack. ______________
5. "These health drinks are **ours**," said Ken and Kathy. ______________
6. **Which** apple should I eat, the green one or the red one? ______________
7. "These bicycles are **theirs**," she said, pointing to Mia and Casey. ______________
8. "Have you eaten **your** five vegetables today?" Mum asked Jordan. ______________

Let's aim high now!

Complete these sentences with a **possessive** or **interrogative pronoun** from the lists you used earlier. The first one has been done for you.

1. These are ____my____ strawberries, not yours.
2. ______________ eats healthier meals—Kiara or Kelvin?
3. That fresh fruit drink is for you, so the drink is ______________.
4. Those exercise bikes belong to me, so the bikes are ______________.
5. Those healthy snacks are for them, so the snacks are ______________.
6. ______________ salad is healthier—the tomato salad or the rice salad?
7. This wholemeal sandwich belongs to her, so the sandwich is ______________.
8. These exercise routines are for us, so the exercise routines are ______________.

Let's put it together now!

These Year 4 students have written seven **pronouns** incorrectly in their advertisement for a health drink. Underline the mistakes and write the words correctly in the spaces below.

Give you health a boost with ours delicious, nutritious Rocket Punch!

Us have used only the freshest fruit, vegetables and herbs to make this amazing drink. Come and try it for youselves. It strong flavour will knock your socks off! Buy some for your friends and family. Them will love you for introducing they to this wonder drink!

____

____

____

____

____

____

____

Let's have fun!

Circle the **pronouns** that are hiding in these words. The first one has been done for you.

Tip! Some words have two **pronouns** hiding in them.

games

health

nourish

cherry

asparagus

cashew

sweet potato

wholemeal

fitter

Let's have a test!

Which sentences have been written correctly?

1
- ◯ Would them like to come with us to the gym?
- ◯ Would her like to come with us to the gym?
- ◯ Would you like to come with us to the gym?
- ◯ Would him like to come with us to the gym?

2
- ◯ They made the salad theirselves.
- ◯ They made the salad theirselfs.
- ◯ They made the salad theyselves.
- ◯ They made the salad themselves.

Which word completes the sentence correctly?

3 Show ______________ how to do the exercises and we will practise them.

◯ us ◯ you ◯ we ◯ they

4 The boy can do the exercises by ______________.

◯ heself ◯ himself ◯ hisself ◯ hiself

Which sentences have been written correctly?

5
- ◯ Mine cereal is healthier than yours.
- ◯ My cereal is healthier than yours.
- ◯ My cereal is healthier than your.
- ◯ Mine cereal is healthier than your.

6
- ◯ What is the fittest person in the class?
- ◯ Whose is the fittest person in the class?
- ◯ Which is the fittest person in the class?
- ◯ Who is the fittest person in the class?

Which word completes the sentence correctly?

7 Tell them to put ______________ hoops next to yours.

◯ you ◯ theirs ◯ their ◯ ours

8 ______________ of the two games would you like to play?

◯ Who ◯ Whose ◯ Which ◯ What

Let's write now!

Create an **advertisement** to persuade people to take up an activity such as walking, running, swimming or playing sport. Avoid repeating nouns too much by using **personal**, **possessive** and **interrogative pronouns** in their place.

Unit 7 Wonders of the world

Focus

Descriptive adjectives; adjectives that compare

The Taj Mahal

When I went with my family to India, we saw a **beautiful** building called the Taj Mahal. It is one of the wonders of the world. In the picture you can see that it stands on a square platform and is made of white marble. The tall towers at each corner are called minarets, and there is a spectacular dome in the centre of the building. Inside, the walls are decorated with many mosaics and semi-precious stones. The Taj Mahal is set in a large garden filled with colourful flowers. There is a long pool in front of the Taj, and you can see the building's reflection in the still water. Our guide told us that it took **twenty** years to build!

by Maddie

This is a **description**. A description helps us form mind pictures of people, places and things. Maddie uses **adjectives** to describe the Taj Mahal.

Adjectives
- are words that describe nouns or pronouns; for example, **beautiful** building.
- tell us how many people, places or things there are; for example, **twenty** years.

Rule! **Adjectives** make our writing more interesting, but only if we use them carefully. Don't use more than three adjectives to describe a noun or pronoun.

Let's find them!

Find these adjectives in the text. Write the adjective that describes the

1. platform ______________________
2. marble ______________________
3. towers ______________________
4. dome ______________________
5. garden ______________________
6. flowers ______________________
7. water ______________________

Let's go to the next step!

We can use adjectives to describe people, places and things in opposite ways. Adjectives that have opposite meanings are called **antonyms**.

The antonyms for these adjectives that describe the wonders of the world are in Column B. Find the matching pairs and shade them the same colour. The first one has been done for you.

Adjective	Antonym
tall	safe
ancient	bottom
first	past
beautiful	short
many	shallow
top	dull
bright	modern
wide	tiny
smooth	last
present	soft
hard	ugly
dangerous	narrow
deep	few
huge	rough

Let's aim high now!

Many adjectives end in **ful**, **less** and **able**. These word endings are called **suffixes**. Complete the adjectives in brackets by adding the correct suffix. For example, Our visit to the Taj Mahal was (wonder) <u>wonderful</u>.

1. The Taj Mahal is set in (peace) ______________________ gardens.
2. We found a (comfort) ______________________ hotel near the ancient ruins.
3. We found the brochure on the Taj Mahal very (help) ______________________.
4. Some (care) ______________________ people dropped litter in the palace courtyard.
5. The water in the pools around the Taj Mahal is not (drink) ______________________.
6. A (knowledge) ______________________ man told us all about the ancient tomb.
7. After I dropped my camera it was (use) ______________________ trying to take photographs.

The Forbidden City

When I went to Beijing, my parents took me to see The Forbidden City. It is one of the most interesting places I've ever been to.

The Forbidden City is one of the largest palaces in the world and was once the home of the Chinese emperors. It is also one of the **most popular** tourist attractions in the world. There is a wall around the palace that is wider at the bottom than at the top. Our guide told us that this made it easier to guard, as it is more difficult to climb a sloping wall than a straight one.

Most of the palace buildings are **grand**, but the ones on the south side are **grander** than those to the north. The Hall of Supreme Harmony is taller and more important than all the other buildings. Many people think it is the **grandest** building in the whole of China, and I agree with them!

by Juan

This is another **description**. Juan uses **adjectives** to compare things in the Forbidden City.

Adjectives can compare people, places and things with each other; for example, **grand**, **grander**, **grandest**. They are called **adjectives of degree**.

Rule!

If two people, places or things are being compared, the adjective usually ends in *er*; for example, **grander**. These are called **comparative adjectives**.

If more than two people, animals, places or things are being compared, the adjective usually ends in *est*; for example, **grandest**. These are called **superlative adjectives**.

When an adjective consists of more than two syllables, we use the word:

- **more** in front of it when comparing two people, places or things; for example, **The Forbidden City is <u>more popular</u> with tourists than the Taj Mahal.**
- **most** in front of it when comparing more than two people, places or things; for example, **The Forbidden City is the <u>most popular</u> tourist attraction of all.**

Let's find them!

Find seven **adjectives of degree** (adjectives that compare) in the text and write them in the spaces below. Remember to look for adjectives that end in *er* and *est*, or that have the words *more* and *most* in front of them. Don't use *grander*, *grandest* or *most popular*.

Tip!

Some adjectives of degree don't follow the usual rules; for example, **good better best** and **bad worse worst**.

1. ______________________
2. ______________________
3. ______________________

4 ______________________________

5 ______________________________

6 ______________________________

7 ______________________________

Let's go to the next step!

Here are some **adjectives** we can use to **compare** wonders of the world. Fill in the missing ones. The first two have been done for you.

Adjective	Comparative (Comparing two)	Superlative (Comparing more than two)	Adjective	Comparative (Comparing two)	Superlative (Comparing more than two)
big	**bigger**	**biggest**	**amazing**	**more amazing**	**most amazing**
pretty			wonderful		
	more fantastic				longest
crowded			enormous		
	shadier			steeper	
magnificent					greatest
	heavier		stunning		

Let's aim high now!

Complete each sentence by writing the **adjective** in brackets in its correct form. For example, Mount Everest is the (high) highest mountain in the world.

1. The pyramids in Egypt are (old) ____________ than the Taj Mahal.
2. We visited the pyramids at the (hot) ____________ time of the year.
3. Of the three statues, that is the (beautiful) ____________.
4. The (good) ____________ place to see corals is at the Great Barrier Reef.
5. This year's trip to Uluru was (enjoyable) ____________ than last year's.
6. Some ancient monuments are (interesting) ____________ than others.
7. Climbing out of the ancient caves was (tiring) ____________ than walking through them.

Let's put it together now!

This student has written seven **adjectives** incorrectly in his description of the Great Pyramid of Giza. Underline the mistakes and write the words correctly in the spaces.

Of the seven wonders of the ancientest world, the Great Pyramid of Giza is the oldest. Some people think it is also the spectacularest. It was the taller building in the world until seven hundred years ago. Because it is a pyramid, it gets narrower and narrowest as it gets towards the top. The south side of the pyramid is the long of the four sides, and the north side is the shorter. The difference in the length of the two sides is only about 15 cm. There are two main chambers inside the pyramid—the King's Chamber and the Queen's Chamber. The King's Chamber is the biggest of the two.

____

____

____

____

____

____

____

Tip!

Pssst! To work out if a word is an adjective or a noun, ask yourself if it can describe a person, place or thing; for example, we can say that someone or something is dangerous, so **dangerous** is an adjective. We can't say that someone or something is journey, so **journey** is a noun.

Let's have fun!

Colour the **adjectives** to get to the Mayan pyramid. Beware of the dangerous nouns around you!

START HERE ↓ (safe)

snake	safe	spider	landslide	thorns	trap	soldiers
spear	refreshing	mosquito	storm	ants	darkness	floods
scorpion	greener	brilliant	cliff	quicksand	thirst	mud
waterfall	vulture	cool	tired	excited	heat	ravine
fire	animals	rocks	accident	special	hunger	mountain

Let's have a test!

Which adjectives complete these sentences correctly?

1. We needed ____________________ time to look around the temple.
   - ◯ more
   - ◯ much
   - ◯ many
   - ◯ most

2. We had to climb ____________________ steps to get to the ancient temple.
   - ◯ lots
   - ◯ many
   - ◯ one
   - ◯ tenth

3. Which adjective does **not** complete this sentence correctly?

   There were ____________________ statues on either side of the gate.
   - ◯ small
   - ◯ stone
   - ◯ obedient
   - ◯ two

4. Which sequence of adjectives does **not** complete this sentence correctly?

   A ______________ guide showed us around the ______________ palace.
   - ◯ friendly, magnificent
   - ◯ magnificent, friendly
   - ◯ massive, huge
   - ◯ huge, massive

Which adjectives complete these sentences correctly?

5. I think that the Taj Mahal is ____________________ than the Great Pyramid.
   - ◯ more beautiful
   - ◯ beautifuller
   - ◯ most beautiful
   - ◯ beautifullest

6. The __________ part of the tour was when I got lost wandering amongst the ruins.
   - ◯ badder
   - ◯ baddest
   - ◯ worse
   - ◯ worst

In which sentences have the adjectives **not** been used correctly?

7. - ◯ The most valuable treasure came from this chamber.
   - ◯ The more valuable treasure came from this chamber.
   - ◯ The valuable treasure came from this chamber.
   - ◯ The valuablest treasure came from this chamber.

8. - ◯ The tunnel we went down was narrower than theirs.
   - ◯ The tunnel we went down was widest than theirs.
   - ◯ The tunnel we went down was longer than theirs.
   - ◯ The tunnel we went down was shorter than theirs.

Let's write now!

Find information on the wonders of the world in books or on the internet. Choose one of them and write a **description** of it. Use **adjectives** to describe and compare people, places and things in your description.

Unit 8 The magical world of animation

Focus
Doing verbs; helping verbs

Kung Fu Panda

One of my favourite animated films is *Kung Fu Panda*. It is about a clumsy, chubby panda called Po who **works** in his father's noodle shop. Secretly, Po would like to be a kung fu master. He gets his wish when the tortoise Master chooses him to fight against the evil snow leopard, Tai Lung. Po's teachers are Shifu, a red panda, and The Five. Shifu discovers that Po has talent and that he learns well when he is rewarded with food. It is not long before Po becomes a skilled warrior. To find out what happens when Po meets Tai Lung, you will have to watch the film.

This film is suitable for people of all ages. It is funny, has great characters, and is full of action. I give it five stars.

by Mark

This is a **review**. A review tells and gives opinions about films, books or shows. Mark uses lots of **doing verbs** to tell what happens in his review of the animated film, *Kung Fu Panda.*

Verbs are the most important words in sentences. They tell us what is happening in the sentence. Without them, sentences don't make sense.

Doing verbs show what people, animal or things do; for example, **works**.

Let's find them!

Find these **doing verbs** in the text that start with these letters.

1. c ______________________________
2. f ______________________________
3. d ______________________________
4. l ______________________________

5 r ______________________________

6 h ______________________________

7 w ______________________________

Let's go to the next step!

Circle the **doing verbs** in these sentences.
For example, The boy (showed) us his collection of DVDs.

Tip!

Psst! Be careful! Some sentences have more than one **doing verb** in them.

1. I laughed all the way through the film.
2. I always buy my cinema tickets online.
3. Sometimes I cry when I watch a sad film.
4. They open the cinema doors at 10 o'clock.
5. We waited in a long queue at the ticket office.
6. I went to the cinema to see the new animated film.
7. The boy who sat next to me in the cinema spilled his popcorn.

Let's aim high now!

Complete each sentence with the correct **doing verb** from the box. Use each verb once.

create	started	marries	gave	waddled	likes
screamed	giggled	walked	told	saw	

1. I ____________________ up the aisle towards my seat.
2. Not everyone ____________________ animated films.
3. At the end of the film, the prince ____________________ the princess.
4. Today our teacher ______________ us how they ______________ animated films.
5. I ________________ my friend some of my chocolates before the film ________________.
6. People in the audience ______________ when they ______________ the monster.
7. My baby sister ____________ when the penguins ______________ onto the screen.

Shrek

I **have** seen all five *Shrek* films, but I think the first one is the best. It is about a disgusting ogre, Shrek, who lives in a smelly swamp in the land of Duloc. One night he wakes up to find that Duloc's fairy tale creatures have set up camp in his swamp. They explain that they are trying to get away from their cruel ruler, Lord Farquaad. Shrek decides that he must go and see this Lord Farquaad. Lord Farquaad tells Shrek that he is looking for a princess to marry so that he can become a king. Shrek says he will help him, on condition that Lord Farquaad gets the fairy tale creatures out of his swamp. The adventure begins when Shrek sets off with a very talkative donkey to find the princess.

If you enjoy a good laugh and like listening to great music, you should watch this film.

by Alicia

This is another **review**. Alicia uses some important **helping verbs** to help other verbs do their work in her review of the animated film, *Shrek*.

Helping verbs are verbs that help other verbs do their work; for example, **have seen**.

These are the helping verbs:

am, **is**, **are**, **was**, **were**, **do**, **does**, **did**, **has**, **have**, **had**, **shall**, **will**, **can**, **may**, **might**, **must**, **could**, **would**, **should**.

Tip!

Tip! If a **verb** consists of more than one word, it is called a **verb group**.

Let's find them!

In the text find the **helping verbs** that make these verbs complete.

1. set up ______________________
2. trying ______________________
3. go ______________________
4. looking ______________________
5. become ______________________
6. help ______________________
7. watch ______________________

Let's go to the next step!

Circle the **helping verbs** in these sentences.

For example, I may buy that DVD to add to my collection of animated films.

1. I will go with you to see the new animated film.
2. You can watch the film, but it may upset you.
3. He is sitting next to my brother in the back row.
4. My friend was watching *Shrek* when I went to visit her.
5. You really must see that animated film about penguins.
6. I am looking forward to going to the cinema with you tomorrow.
7. I could tell you how the film ends, but that would spoil it for you.

Tip!

Psst! Be careful! Some sentences have more than one **helping verb** in them.

Let's aim high now!

Sometimes there is another word between a verb and its helper; for example, He is not watching the film. Find the **verb group** in each sentence and write it in the space.

For example, He is not watching that film. is watching

1. He will never watch that film! ______________________
2. He has never been to a cinema. ______________________
3. They were not waiting for us at the cinema. ______________________
4. I have often seen that boy at the local cinema. ______________________
5. Mum will sometimes let us watch a DVD before bedtime. ______________________
6. Little children should not go to the cinema by themselves. ______________________
7. You must always take your litter with you when you leave the cinema.

____

Let's put it together now!

This student has left out these **doing** and **helping verbs** in her review of the animated film, *Finding Nemo*.

have   are   lives   will   recommend   captures   escape

Can you help her fill them in?

One of my favourite animated films is *Finding Nemo*. It is about a little clownfish called Nemo, who ________________ with his father on the Great Barrier Reef. One day, a scuba diver ________________ Nemo. Nemo ends up in a small aquarium in a dentist's room. While his father and a fish called Dory ________________ looking everywhere for him, Nemo tries to ________________.

If you ________________ not watched this film, I ________________ that you do. I don't think it ________________ spoil it for you if I tell you that it has a happy ending.

Let's have fun!

1. The verbs scattered around this scene from an animated film tell us what the characters are doing. Use lines to join each **verb** to the character that is performing the action.

flies
catches
hops
cries
eats

paints
laughs
drinks
blows
reads

2. Make these **helping verbs** fit into the spaces in the puzzle.

should
would
have
has
can
are
did
will

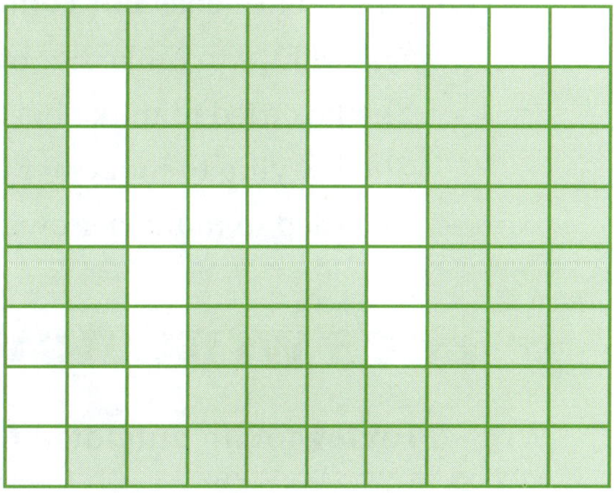

Let's have a test!

Which words complete the sentences correctly?

1. I always ______________________ carefully to what the characters are saying.

   ◯ hear ◯ watch ◯ listen ◯ see

2. I often ______________________ a DVD from my friend.

   ◯ lend ◯ watch ◯ borrow ◯ see

Which words do **not** complete the sentences correctly?

3. The artist ______________________ pictures that are used in animations.

   ◯ draws ◯ writes ◯ paints ◯ creates

4. The child ______________________ her cool drink in the foyer.

   ◯ spilled ◯ sipped ◯ left ◯ sent

Which words complete the sentences correctly?

5. He ______________________ not want to see the new animated film.

   ◯ were ◯ does ◯ have ◯ was

6. I said I ______________________ buy the ticket for him.

   ◯ would ◯ do
   ◯ has ◯ am

7. Which sentence contains a helping verb?

   ◯ They go to the cinema once a week.
   ◯ They enjoy going to the cinema once a week.
   ◯ They might go to the cinema once a week.
   ◯ They used to go to the cinema once a week.

8. Which sentence does **not** contain a helping verb?

   ◯ She will try to make her own animated film.
   ◯ She has tried to make her own animated film.
   ◯ She is trying to make her own animated film.
   ◯ She tried to make her own animated film.

Let's write now!

Write a **review** of an animated film that you have watched. Use **doing** and **helping verbs** in your review.

Unit 9 Festivals and holidays

Focus

Saying, thinking and feeling verbs; "being" and "having" verbs

Stacey's diary

30 October

Dear Diary

I'm so excited. Tomorrow is Halloween. Mum **says** I can go trick-or-treating at Springfield Village with Lisa, Lan and Suzie. I'm going to **ask** Julie to come too. I hope the treats are as good as they were last year. Mum's just announced that she's coming too! She **figures** it's safer that way. If I **remember** correctly, she found an excuse to come with us last year as well. I think she just wants some of our lollies. I **wish** I had something scarier to wear than a witch's costume. I really **enjoy** scaring people. Lisa reckons she's got the scariest costume, but Lan's seen it and she told me it's not that scary. I think I'll tell Mum to dangle some spiders around the brim of my witch's hat. Lisa always screams when she sees a spider! And if they don't scare anyone else, at least they'll keep the flies off my face.

I can't wait until tomorrow. I love Halloween!

This is a **diary entry**. A diary entry is a record people keep of things that are happening or have happened to them. Stacey uses **saying verbs** to express different ways people say things and **thinking** and **feeling verbs** to express thoughts and emotions while telling about Halloween.

Saying verbs are doing verbs that express different ways of saying or communicating; for example, **says, ask**.

Thinking verbs are doing verbs that express different ways of thinking or using our brains; for example, **figures, remember**.

Feeling verbs are doing verbs that express emotions; for example, **wish, enjoy**.

Let's find them!

Find the **saying, thinking** and **feeling verbs** in the text that start with these letters.

Saying verbs

1. a________________
2. t________________
3. s________________

Thinking verbs

4. t________________
5. r________________

Feeling verbs

6. h________________
7. l________________

Let's go to the next step!

Read the sentences below carefully and then circle the **saying verbs**, put a box around the **thinking verbs** and underline the **feeling verbs**; for example:

"What a great witch's hat!" she exclaimed.

I will consider going with him to the festival.

The child panicked when she saw me in my skeleton costume.

1. I like dressing up for Halloween.
2. I wonder if we'll go trick-or-treating this year.
3. It annoys me when people don't behave at festivals.
4. We all gasped when they threw the acrobat into the air.
5. Everyone remarked on how beautiful the floats were this year.
6. People cheered when the festival queen walked onto the stage.
7. I guessed how many lollies there were in the jar and won an iPod.

Let's aim high now!

Complete each sentence with a **saying**, **thinking** or **feeling verb** from the box. State what kind of verb it is in the space next to each sentence.

For example, My little brother groaned when we told him we were going to the festival. saying verb

fascinates	remember	shouted	grumbled
discussed	irritates	imagine	

Tip! Psst! Use each word once.

1. I ____________ the arrangements for my party with my mum. ____________
2. It ____________ me to see how other people celebrate Christmas. ____________
3. The man next to me ____________ that he couldn't see the stage. ____________
4. Do you ____________ what you got for your birthday last year? ____________
5. I ____________ for joy when our team won the dragon boat race. ____________
6. I ____________ there must be many different ways of celebrating the arrival of spring. ____________
7. It ____________ me when he boasts about all the lollies he got for Halloween. ____________

Jarred's diary

5 May

Here I **am** in Korea! It was great to see Joon again. Today is Children's Day, and Joon's mum and dad invited us to lunch. Joon says they always **have** a special family lunch on Children's Day. Afterwards we all went to the zoo. We had a great time, even though there were crowds of people there. Joon told me that Children's Day has been a national holiday in Korea since 1978. Many Koreans give their children presents on Children's Day. Joon got a really cool tablet. He already has lots of apps on it.

Joon's mum and dad said he can visit me in Australia in July. We are so excited. It will be fun for him to see his other friends again. He misses his Australian school.

I'd better go now. We have a busy day planned for tomorrow and I must go to bed early.

This is another **diary entry**. Jarred uses **being verbs** to show that people or things exist and **having verbs** to show what people have while telling about how he spent Children's Day in Korea.

Being verbs show that people or things exist; for example, **Here I <u>am</u> in Korea.**

Having verbs show what people or things have; for example, **Joon says they always <u>have</u> a special family lunch on Children's Day.**

Rule!

- The **being** verbs are **am, is, are, was, were, be, being** and **been.**
- The **having** verbs are **has, had** and **have.**

Tip!

Tip! The verbs **be, being** and **been** are only used with other verbs; for example, **will be, are being, has been.**

Let's find them!

Find seven **being** and **having verbs** in the text and write them in the spaces. Don't use the ones in bold.

1. ______________________________

2. ______________________________

3. ______________________________

4. ______________________________

5. ______________________________

6. ______________________________

7. ______________________________

Let's go to the next step!

Circle the **being** and **having verbs** in these sentences; for example, Children's Day (is) a national holiday in Korea.

1. We will be in Korea for the New Year celebrations.
2. I have been to the Lotus Lantern Festival in Korea.
3. I am at the stadium where the parade will take place.
4. There were lots of people in the park on Children's Day.
5. There are lots of festivals in the world that I don't know about.
6. It has been fun to see the different costumes people wear at festivals.
7. I have pleasant memories of spending Children's Day with Joon's family.

Let's aim high now!

Choose a **being** or **having verb** from the box to complete each sentence. Use each word once.

has	is	was	been	were	are	be

1. My favourite holiday ____________________ Christmas.
2. He has ____________________ to many Dragon Boat festivals.
3. Joon ____________________ a photo of himself doing the Lion Dance.
4. That ____________________ the best Spring Carnival I've ever been to!
5. Lots of people are going to ____________________ at the festival next week.
6. There ____________________ presents for many children on Children's Day.
7. They ____________________ upset because they have missed the most important part of the ceremony.

Let's put it together now!

This student has left out these **verbs** in his diary entry about St Patrick's Day:

thought	are	explained	was	is	had	enjoyed

Can you help him fill them in?

18th March

Ireland ________________ great, and so ________________ Dad's Irish relatives. We're staying with them for a few days. Yesterday ________________ St Patrick's Day. Aunt Maud took us into town to watch the St Patrick's Day Parade. Shaun ________________ it was boring, but I ________________ it. Most of the people were wearing something green, especially bunches of shamrocks. Aunt Maud ________________ that the shamrock is the symbol of Ireland. Some of the people in the parade ________________ on green leprechaun suits. They looked hilarious.

Let's have fun!

At many festivals in Mexico, someone breaks a piñata and lollies, fruit or small toys come pouring out.

See if you can put the lollies from this piñata into the correct packets.

Let's have a test!

1. Which sentence contains a saying verb?
   - ◯ He wanted to watch the parade.
   - ◯ He liked watching the parade.
   - ◯ He was pleased that he had watched the parade.
   - ◯ He replied that he had watched the parade.

2. Which sentence contains a thinking verb?
   - ◯ I have never been to a snow festival.
   - ◯ I said I would go to the snow festival.
   - ◯ I love going to snow festivals!
   - ◯ I sometimes wonder if I will ever go to a snow festival.

3. Which sentence contains a feeling verb?
   - ◯ She cheered up when the parade started.
   - ◯ She cheered for the people in the parade.
   - ◯ She was cheerful once the parade started.
   - ◯ She heard the cheers for the people in the parade.

4. Which word completes this sentence correctly?

   They ____________________ us to stay away from the stage.
   - ◯ admired
   - ◯ noticed
   - ◯ warned
   - ◯ forgot

5. Which word does **not** complete this sentence correctly?

   I ____________________ there will be lots of people at the festival.
   - ◯ know
   - ◯ suppose
   - ◯ think
   - ◯ frighten

6. Which being verb completes this sentence correctly?

   There ____________________ thousands of spectators at the Children's Day celebration.
   - ◯ was
   - ◯ were
   - ◯ is
   - ◯ be

7. Which sentence contains a having verb?
   - ◯ The marchers are playing bagpipes.
   - ◯ The marchers will play bagpipes.
   - ◯ Some of the marchers had bagpipes.
   - ◯ Some of the marchers are going to play bagpipes.

8. Which verb completes this sentence correctly.

   She has ____________________ to lots of spring festivals before.
   - ◯ be
   - ◯ being
   - ◯ been

Let's write now!

Which is your favourite festival or holiday? Write an entry in your diary telling what you did or what you plan to do on that day. Try to use some **being** and **having verbs** and at least one **saying verb**, one **thinking verb** and one **feeling verb** in your **diary entry**.

Unit 10 Exploring the unknown

Focus

Verbs—tense

Exploring new lands

Today we **know** that the world is round. At this moment, people **are travelling** from one end of the earth to the other. Long ago, however, people thought the earth was flat. They believed that if they sailed too far from land, they would fall off the edge. This **stopped** them from exploring the oceans and finding new lands. Then, about 600 years ago, the Portuguese started to build stronger ships, and this **gave** them the confidence to sail further into the oceans. They **went** right around Africa and eventually made their way to India.

At about the same time, Christopher Columbus **was trying** to reach India by sailing across the Atlantic Ocean. He landed in America instead!

Before long, explorers were sailing to the four corners of the earth. One of them, Captain James Cook, reached the south east coast of Australia in 1770. Eighteen years later, the first white settlers arrived in Sydney Cove.

by Jeremy

This is a **recount**. Remember—a recount tells about things that have already happened. Jeremy uses mainly **past tense verbs** to tell about explorers who sailed across the oceans long ago.

Tense in verbs tells us when something happens.

Present tense verbs show that actions happen at this time; for example, **know**. If the action might end soon, the **–ing** form of the verb is used with the helpers **is** and **are**; for example, **are travelling**.

Past tense verbs show that actions have already happened; for example, **stopped**.

Some **past tense** verbs show that an action was happening at a particular time. They use the **–ing** form of the verb with the helpers **was** or **were**; for example, **was trying**.

Rule!

- Many past tense verbs are formed by adding *ed*; for example, **stop → stopped**.
- Other past tense verbs are formed by changing the spelling; for example, **give → gave**.
- Some verbs change altogether when written in the past tense; for example, **go → went**.
- Verbs that show a continuous action change the tense of the verb *be*; for example, **is trying/are trying** change to **was trying/were trying**.

Let's find them!

Find these **past tense verbs** in the text.

1. think ______________________

2. is ______________________________

3. sail ______________________________

4. start ______________________________

5. are sailing ______________________________

6. reach ______________________________

7. arrive ______________________________

Let's go to the next step!

Circle the **past tense verbs** in these sentences.
For example, Captain James Cook (sailed) to many different lands.

1. Many explorers died in foreign lands.
2. The early explorers spent many months at sea.
3. Captain Cook's ship scraped the Great Barrier Reef.
4. Some European countries were hoping to find new lands.
5. Many people think that the early explorers were very brave men.
6. The explorer was crossing the Antarctic Circle when he saw the iceberg.
7. James Cook mapped the New Zealand and eastern Australian coastlines in 1870.

Let's aim high now!

Write the verbs in brackets in the **past tense**.
Use a dictionary to help you with the spellings.

1. Christopher Columbus (goes) ________________ to America four times.
2. Many early explorers (are) ________________ afraid of sailing into the unknown.
3. Matthew Flinders (is) ________________ the first man to sail right around Australia.
4. Some early explorers in Australia (disappear) ________________ without trace.
5. Charles Sturt (journey) ________________ to northern New South Wales at the beginning of the 19th century.
6. Gregory Blaxland, William Lawson and William Wentworth (find) ________________ a way across the Blue Mountains.
7. While some settlers (are making) ________________ attempts to reach the interior of Australia, others (are settling) ________________ around the coast.

Exploring space

More than thirty years ago, the Americans sent two unmanned spacecraft, Voyager 1 and Voyager 2, into space to explore the solar system. The Voyagers are sending information back to Earth, but their power and fuel **are going to run out** in 2020. By then they will be about 17 billion kilometres from the sun.

In the next twenty or thirty years, the Voyager spacecraft are going to leave the solar system and **will continue** to float through space. Eventually they will pass other stars. Voyager 1 will reach the first of these stars in 40 000 years' time!

Although scientists don't know for sure what will happen to the Voyagers, they think they will wander through the Milky Way galaxy forever—if they don't crash into anything! Attached to each spacecraft is a disc that contains information about Earth. If extra-terrestrials ever find the spacecraft, they will learn something about Earth by watching the images and listening to the sounds on the discs.

by Judy

This is a **report**. Remember—a report provides information and facts. Judy uses mainly **future tense verbs** to show that actions are still going to happen while telling about the Voyager spacecraft.

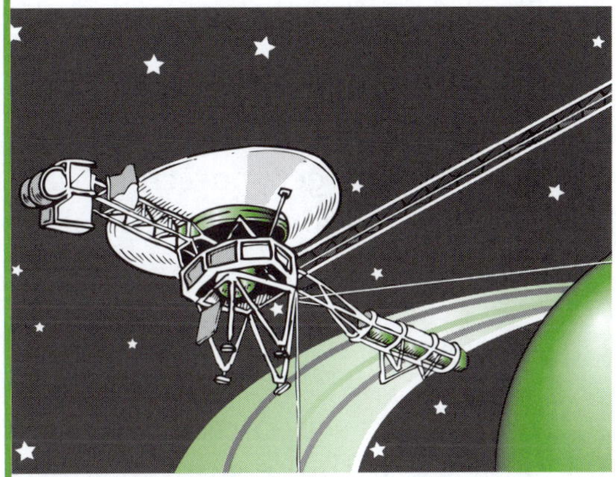

Future tense verbs

- show that actions are still going to happen; for example, **are going to run out**.
- can also contain the helping **verb** will; for example, **will continue**.

Let's find them!

Find the **future tense** of these verbs in the text.

1. are ______________________
2. leave ______________________
3. pass ______________________
4. reach ______________________
5. happen ______________________
6. wander ______________________
7. learn ______________________

Let's go to the next step!

Complete each sentence with a **future tense** verb group from the box.
Use each verb group once.

is going to replace	are going to be	will start	will establish
will know	are going to join	are going to send back	

1. The astronauts ________________ their training tomorrow.
2. There ________________ other expeditions to the moon.
3. Perhaps humans ________________ a settlement on the moon.
4. A new crew of astronauts ________________ the old crew.
5. Scientists believe that soon they ________________ more about the solar system.
6. Two more astronauts ________________ the crew on the International Space Station.
7. The Voyager spacecraft ________________ more information about the solar system.

Let's aim high now!

Write these sentences in the **future tense**. Use either **going to** or **will**. Start each sentence with the word or words you have been given.

For example: They have voted to cancel the mission to Mars.
Tomorrow they **will vote** to cancel the mission to Mars. OR
Tomorrow they **are going to vote** to cancel the mission to Mars.

1. They check the spacecraft carefully. Next week ________________
____
2. Scientists study soil and rocks from the moon. Next month ________________
____
3. We visit the observatory to learn about space. Next Friday ________________
____
4. The spacecraft sends information back to Earth.
Next year ________________
____
5. They launch the spacecraft if the weather is clear.
Tomorrow morning ________________
____
6. Astronauts train for a long time before they go into space.
In the future, ________________
____
7. Astronauts on the International Space Station conduct experiments.
Soon, ________________
____

Let's put it together now!

This student has written the **verbs** in bold in the wrong tense. Write them correctly in the spaces.

Ships **are** ____________________ sailing to Antarctica as early as the 19th century. In the 1890s, many explorers **go** ____________________ to Antarctica, but they **find** ____________________ the conditions very harsh. Finally, on 14th December 1911, the Norwegian, Roald Amundsen, **reach** ____________________ the South Pole.

These days, many countries **sent** ____________________ scientists to Antarctica to study such things as the weather, plant and animal life and glaciers. Some of these scientists have discovered a large lake hidden beneath Antarctica's ice sheet. They plan to do a survey of the area first, then they **drill** ____________________ down into the lake. After that they **explore** ____________________ and sample the lake water.

Let's have fun!

Sort the verbs and verb groups in the box into **past**, **present** and **future tense** verbs, and then write them in the correct place.

The **past tense** verbs belong with the old sailing ship, the **present tense** verbs belong with the motor car, and the **future tense** verbs belong with the spacecraft.

was discovering	sank	were trading	brake
travel	landed	speeds	are going to find
will fly	is going to fix	swam	is going to explore
saw	steers	will record	
arrive	will photograph	stops	

Past tense

Present tense

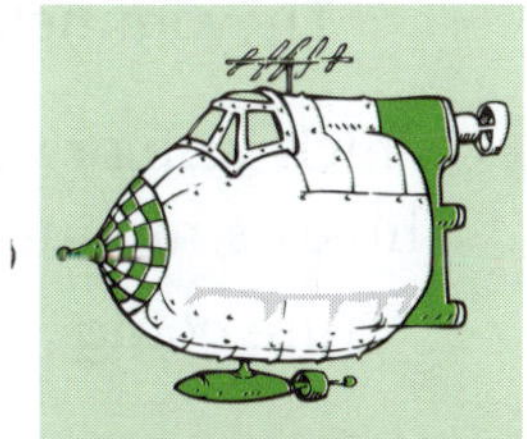

Future tense

Let's have a test!

Which sentences have been written correctly?

1
- ◯ Yesterday I watched a program about space exploration.
- ◯ Yesterday I watch a program about space exploration.
- ◯ Yesterday I will watch a program about space exploration.
- ◯ Yesterday I am going to watch a program about space exploration.

2
- ◯ I wrote a recount about Captain Cook tomorrow.
- ◯ I was writing a recount about Captain Cook tomorrow.
- ◯ I have been writing a recount about Captain Cook tomorrow.
- ◯ I will write a recount about Captain Cook tomorrow.

3 Which verb or verb group completes this sentence correctly?

The explorers ______________________ to find new lands.

◯ were hoping ◯ was hoping ◯ hoping ◯ hopes

4 Which verb does **not** complete this sentence correctly?

Captain Cook ______________________ to many new lands.

◯ journeyed ◯ travelled ◯ voyaged ◯ sail

Which sentences have been written **incorrectly**?

5
- ◯ The spaceship will reach Saturn.
- ◯ The spaceship reach Saturn.
- ◯ The spaceship reached Saturn.
- ◯ The spaceship has reached Saturn.

6
- ◯ They are going to launch the spaceship next month.
- ◯ They will launch the spaceship next month.
- ◯ They launch the spaceship next month.
- ◯ They launched the spaceship next month.

7 Which verb or verb group completes this sentence correctly?

Three astronauts ______________________ to the moon next year.

◯ are going ◯ was going ◯ gone ◯ goes

8 Which verb does **not** complete this sentence correctly?

In the future, more astronauts ______________________ to the moon.

◯ will travel ◯ travelled ◯ may travel ◯ are going to travel

Let's write now!

Choose one of the following options:

- Research the life of a famous explorer and write a **recount** about one of his expeditions OR
- Choose a planet to research, and then write a **report** about it.

Unit 11 Ways of communicating

Focus
Adverbs; phrases and prepositions

This is an **explanation**. An explanation tells how things work or why they happen. Amy uses **adverbs** to add meaning to verbs while explaining how sign language works.

Sign language

Before humans developed spoken language, they used sign language to communicate with each other. When we talk about sign language today, we usually think of the way deaf people are able to understand and communicate information. However, we all use sign language occasionally. Have you ever waved hello or goodbye to someone? You were using sign language!

People who are deaf are generally unable to communicate verbally. They, and the people they live and work with, communicate by signing.

Each country has its own sign alphabet. Most people are able to learn the sign alphabet easily, but stringing the letters together quickly to make words is more difficult. If you want to sign fluently, you have to keep practising.

by Amy

Adverbs add meaning to verbs by telling

- how something is done; for example, **She spoke excitedly.**
- where something is done; for example, **She spoke inside.**
- when something is done; for example, **She spoke immediately.**
- to what extent something is done; for example, **She hardly spoke.**
- how often something is done; for example, **She spoke often.**

Tip!
Many **adverbs**, especially those that tell how something is done, end in **ly**.

Let's find them!

Find seven **adverbs** that end in *ly* in the text and write them in the spaces.

1 ______________________

2 ______________________

3 ______________________

4. ______________________________

5. ______________________________

6. ______________________________

7. ______________________________

Let's go to the next step!

Find an **adverb** in the box to complete each sentence. The word in brackets at the end of the sentence tells you what kind of adverb to look for. Use each adverb once.

clearly	carefully	away	excitedly	afterwards	upwards	soon

1. The sign said DANGER, so we kept ______________. (Where)
2. He wrote the message ______________ on special paper. (How)
3. Our coach said he would speak to us ______________. (When)
4. She said she would ______________ be ready to use sign language. (When)
5. Everyone could hear her because she spoke so ______________. (How)
6. His thumb was pointing ______________, so we knew his team had won. (Where)
7. He announced ______________ that he had something important to tell us. (How)

Let's aim high now!

Underline the **adverb** in each sentence and fill in whether it tells **when**, **where** or **how** the action is done.

For example: She told me to put the sign alphabet chart <u>down</u>. (where)

1. We arrived early for the performance. ______________
2. She waited tensely for her turn to speak. ______________
3. He phoned to say he would meet us later. ______________
4. The teacher gestured to him to move forward. ______________
5. They ran inside when they saw the flash of lightning. ______________
6. He moved his arms apart to indicate how big the fish was. ______________
7. We clapped loudly to show how much we enjoyed the show. ______________

The telephone

Alexander Graham Bell invented the telephone in 1876 and, **for the first time**, people were able to speak to each other across long distances. So how does this amazing invention work?

When you dial or punch in a number on your landline phone, electrical signals are sent through wires or cables to the telephone exchange. From there, the signals are directed to the other phone, causing it to ring. When the other person answers the phone, their voice vibrates into the mouthpiece, where a disc turns the voice sounds into electrical signals. These signals travel along wires to your phone, and a disc in the earpiece of your phone turns the electrical signals back into sounds. Then when you speak into the mouthpiece of your phone, the same thing happens in reverse.

by Joshua

This is another **explanation**. Joshua uses **phrases** to add important detail to sentences while explaining how a telephone works.

Phrases
- are groups of words that add important information or detail to sentences.
- do not contain a verb.

Adverbial phrases do the work of adverbs; for example, **for the first time** tells when people were able to speak to each other over long distances.

Let's find them!

Find these phrases in the text.

Write the phrase that tells us:

1. when Alexander Graham Bell invented the telephone. ______
2. where people were able to speak to each other. ______
3. where you dial or punch in a phone number. ______
4. where electrical signals are sent. ______
5. where the other person's voice vibrates. ______
6. where these signals travel. ______
7. where the disc is. ______

Let's go to the next step!

Prepositions

- are important little words that tell us about the position of people or things.
- often come at the beginning of an adverbial phrase; for example, **for the first time**.

Prepositions			
about	behind	for	since
above	below	from	through
across	beneath	in	to
after	beside	into	under
around	by	of	until
at	down	on	up
before	during	over	with

Circle the **prepositions** in these sentences.

For example, The telephone is in the study.

1. We've had this radio since April.
2. I sent a postcard to my aunt and uncle.
3. My brother got a mobile phone for his birthday.
4. We lost the signal on our television during the storm.
5. I made lots of phone calls to my friends this morning.
6. My cat walked over the keyboard while I was typing an email.
7. When I need information about something, I usually look on the internet.

Tip!

Psst! Some sentences contain more than one **preposition**.

Let's aim high now!

Complete the **phrase** in each sentence with a **preposition** from the box above.

For example: My favourite TV program is **on the other channel**.

1. Our TV aerial is ______________________ **the roof**.
2. Last night I went to bed ______________________ **the news**.
3. My phone has never rung **late** ______________________ **night**.
4. We have three television sets ______________________ **our house**.
5. We live ______________________ **the road** from a mobile phone tower.
6. My grandparents were happy to receive a card ______________________ **me**.
7. My mother moved the computer so that she could dust ______________________ **it**.

Let's put it together now!

This student has left out these **adverbs** and **prepositions** in his explanation. Can you fill them in for him?

invisibly   across   daily   through   quickly   from   instantly

How radio works

Most of us listen to the radio ____________, but have you ever wondered how the sounds get to us ____________ the radio station?

When the announcers speak or play music, the sounds are carried ____________ through the air on radio waves. These waves can pass ____________ solid objects. They also travel very ____________, so we hear them almost ____________ as the antennas on our radios pick up their signal. Radio waves can transmit conversations, music, pictures and other information ____________ millions of kilometres. They can even transmit signals through outer space!

Let's have fun!

Use the sign language alphabet to help you decode the **adverbs** and **prepositions** in these sentences. Write the answers in the spaces next to the sentences.

1. The contestant smiled  when the TV announcer told him he had won the big prize. ____________

2. I was having dinner  my family when I heard the news  the radio. ____________

3. The actors played their parts , and  the end of the show, the audience clapped .
____

4. , people used smoke signals to send messages  long distances.
____

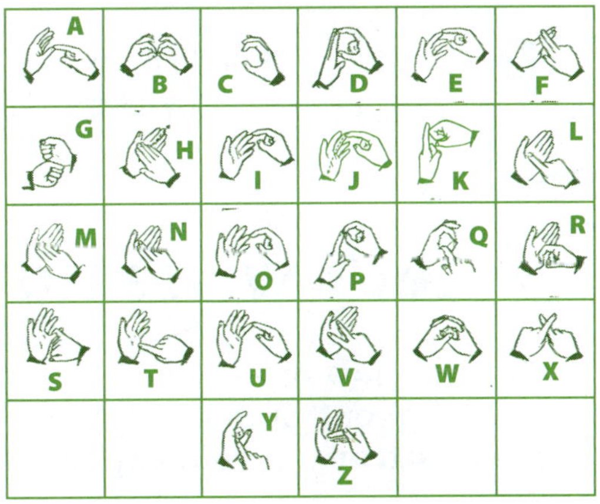

Let's have a test!

1. Which sentence tells when she made the phone call?
   - ◯ She made the phone call indoors.
   - ◯ She made the phone call earlier.
   - ◯ She made the phone call on the bus.
   - ◯ She made the phone call nervously.

2. Which sentence tells where they are listening to the news?
   - ◯ They are listening to the news now.
   - ◯ They are listening to the news excitedly.
   - ◯ They are listening to the news in the car.
   - ◯ They are listening to the news with interest.

3. Which sentence tells how he announced the winner?
   - ◯ He announced the winner clearly.
   - ◯ He announced the winner at the assembly.
   - ◯ He announced the winner yesterday.
   - ◯ He announced the winner last week.

Which words complete these sentences correctly?

4. The children were watching television ______________________.
   - ◯ quiet
   - ◯ quietly
   - ◯ quieter
   - ◯ quietest

5. She contacted her friend ______________________ email.
   - ◯ for
   - ◯ by
   - ◯ since
   - ◯ around

6. He handed the phone ______________________ his friend.
   - ◯ towards
   - ◯ over
   - ◯ to
   - ◯ beneath

Which words do **not** complete these sentences correctly?

7. The television was ______________________ the table.
   - ◯ on
   - ◯ under
   - ◯ above
   - ◯ until

8. I found my mobile phone ______________________ the door.
   - ◯ behind
   - ◯ by
   - ◯ between
   - ◯ beside

Let's write now!

Find out how one of these forms of communication works: the telegraph, television, mobile phone or internet. Write an **explanation** of how it works. Use **adverbs** and **prepositions** in your explanation.

Unit 12 Let's get creative!

Focus
Adjectival phrases; noun groups

A picture of nature

Last week I created a painting **of nature** using acrylic paints. In my painting, there is a gum tree with shady branches. Beside the gum tree is a pond, and leaves from the tree are lying on the ground. A lizard without a tail is climbing up the tree. A kookaburra on a branch is eyeing a frog beside the pond. A fox beneath the tree is also looking at the frog.

by Amelia

This is a **description**. Remember, a description helps us form mind pictures of people, places and things. Amelia uses **adjectival phrases** to give more information about nouns while describing her painting.

Adjectival phrases
- do the work of adjectives by giving more information about nouns; for example, **of nature** describes a painting.
- start with a preposition; for example, **of**.

Let's find them!

Find these **adjectival phrases** in the text.

Write the adjectival phrase that describes the

1. gum tree ______
2. leaves ______
3. lizard ______
4. kookaburra ______
5. frog ______
6. fox ______

Let's go to the next step!

Complete each **adjectival phrase** with a **preposition** from the box. Use each preposition once.

of	inside	about	with	above	on	in

1. I made a cat ____________________ pointy ears out of clay.
2. I found a book ____________________ famous artists at the library.
3. Gran gave me a box ____________________ pastels for my birthday.
4. The painting ____________________ the antique table is very valuable.
5. The paintbrushes ____________________ the table need to be washed.
6. The box ____________________ the cupboard is full of arts and crafts items.
7. My great-grandfather made the rocking horse that sits ____________________ my bedroom.

Let's aim high now!

Complete each sentence with an **adjectival phrase** from the box.
Use each phrase once.

in the city	without an arm	on the walls	around that box
from the balcony	with talent	across the road	

1. Now there is an artist ______________________________!
2. The paintings ______________________________ are magnificent!
3. The ribbon ______________________________ is very decorative.
4. The artist painted the view ______________________________.
5. Our friends ______________________________ often go to the art gallery.
6. The house ______________________________ has lots of statues in the garden.
7. I dropped the glass figure and now it is a lady ______________________________.

Making a robot

You will need:

One large box, a smaller box, two toilet roll tubes, **a long cardboard tube**, two plastic containers, **a roll of aluminium foil**, scissors, sticky tape, a glue stick and scraps of card or paper.

Attach the small box to the bigger box with tape to form the head and body.

Cut the long tube in two. Make a hole on each side of the big box and insert the tubes. Secure with tape.

Cut a length of cardboard slightly longer than the width of the big box. Attach it to the bottom of the box. Attach the toilet roll tubes to the cardboard, and the plastic containers to the toilet roll tubes (see picture).

Cover the entire robot with aluminium foil.

Create an interesting face for your robot from the scraps of card or paper.

by Cheng

This is a **procedure**. A procedure tells how to make or do something. Cheng uses **noun groups** to tell what is involved in making a robot.

Noun groups

- are groups of words that are built around nouns. They include information about the person or thing being spoken or written about; for example, the noun group, **a long cardboard tube**, gives important information about the **tube**.
- can have the articles **a**, **an** or **the**; a pronoun; and one or more adjectives before the noun; for example, **a long cardboard tube**.
- can have one or more adjectival phrases after the noun; for example, **a roll of aluminium foil**.

Let's find them!

Find these **noun groups** in the text.
The noun group that is built around the noun

1. box ______
2. tubes ______
3. containers ______
4. stick ______
5. scraps ______

6. robot ______________________________

7. face ______________________________

Let's go to the next step!

Circle the **noun groups** in these sentences.

For example, I have made (a big, silver robot with floppy arms.)

1. I might use those red beads in the blue box.
2. I kept the two little pictures from the exhibition.
3. Mum wove that pretty basket next to the table.
4. He liked the colourful border around my picture.
5. I am going to decorate that clay pot on the shelf.
6. Please pass me those long pieces of coloured wire.
7. She has written an exciting book about lost treasure.

Let's aim high now!

Complete each sentence with a **noun group** from the box. Use each **noun group** once.

that large house across the road
a beautiful necklace of precious stones
the tall vase on the dining room table
a poodle with a fancy collar
my idea for that painting
Some of the sculptures in the museum
that iron horseshoe above the door

1. A blacksmith made ______________________________
____
2. ______________________________
______________________________ are very valuable.
3. At the dog show, I saw ______________________________
4. An architect designed ______________________________
5. My grandmother arranged the tulips in ______________________________
____
6. I got ______________________________
______________________________ from a picture I saw in a magazine.
7. My mother has ______________________________
______________________________ that she wears on special occasions.

Let's put it together now!

These important words are missing from the **adjectival phrases** and **noun groups** in this student's description. Can you fill them in for her?

of	curvy	my	strands	about	with	an

This is ________________ favourite puppet. She has a round head, ________________ the size of a tennis ball. A square ________________ white cotton fabric covers her head and drapes down to form her body. ________________ elastic band holds the fabric in place beneath her head. She has big blue eyes ________________ long black lashes, a small nose, ________________ red lips and hair made from ________________ of wool. Her name is Pippa.

Let's have fun!

Complete these noun groups with **adjectival phrases** from the box.

1 
the old-fashioned painting
____
____

2 
the big circle
____
____

3 
the little girl
____
____

4 
the modern statue
____
____

5 
the scented candles
____
____

6 
a large can
____
____

7 
a white rose
____
____

8 
the old paintbrush
____
____

of green paint
without any bristles
from the bouquet
on the table
in the top left-hand corner
with the crazy hairstyle
in the fancy frame
between the two lamps

Let's have a test!

Which words complete the sentences correctly?

1 A painting ______________ the collection is on show at the gallery.

- ◯ against
- ◯ from
- ◯ through
- ◯ for

2 The girl ______________ long curly hair is an excellent pianist.

- ◯ of
- ◯ about
- ◯ by
- ◯ with

Which words do **not** complete the sentences correctly?

3 My model is the one ______________ the cupboard.

- ◯ among
- ◯ inside
- ◯ beside
- ◯ on

4 The decorations ______________ the window are all handmade.

- ◯ above
- ◯ beneath
- ◯ near
- ◯ during

5 Which word completes this sentence correctly?

In the middle of the picture was ______________ oval shape with spots on it.

- ◯ two
- ◯ an
- ◯ some
- ◯ a

Which phrases complete the sentences correctly?

6 I noticed ______________ on the box.

- ◯ an large metal clasp
- ◯ many large metal clasp
- ◯ a large metal clasp
- ◯ those large metal clasp

7 The fountain ______________ is very old.

- ◯ in the park
- ◯ about the park
- ◯ among the park
- ◯ between the park

8 Which sentence has been written correctly?

- ◯ My uncle sculpted the bronze tall statue at the bottom of the garden.
- ◯ My uncle sculpted the tall bronze statue at the bottom of the garden.
- ◯ My uncle the tall bronze statue at the bottom of the garden sculpted.
- ◯ My uncle sculpted at the bottom of the garden the bronze tall statue.

Let's write now!

Choose one of the following to write about:

- Find a picture in a book or magazine, or on the internet, and write a **description** of it OR
- Write a **procedure** that tells how to make something.

Use **adjectival phrases** and **noun groups** in your description or procedure.

Unit 13 The seasons

Focus

Commas; contractions; apostrophes that show ownership

Summer

Summer's here at last!
It's my favourite time of the year.
It's **the beach, swimming and picnics**.
It's shorts, tee-shirts and thongs.
It's school holidays, presents and fireworks.
It's iced drinks, ice-cream and ice lollies.
It's when I get to eat my favourite fruits—
plums, peaches and juicy berries.
It's when I don't have to wear woollen jumpers.
It's when I **won't** eat hot soup for dinner!
And I really can't bear to have long hair
When the sun's hot and makes my neck sticky.
So let's all have fun, and play in the sun
In our shorts, tee-shirts and thongs.

by Connor

This is a **poem**. A poem uses words in imaginative ways to express ideas or to describe people or things. Connor uses **commas** to separate items in lists, and **apostrophes** to shorten words and make them easier to say in this poem about summer.

Commas are used to separate

- nouns in a list; for example, **the beach, swimming and picnics**.
- adjectives in a list; for example, **rough, wild and windy weather**.
- a list of actions; for example, **they swam, looked for shells and built sandcastles**.

Tip!

The conjunctions **and** and **or** are usually used instead of a comma to separate the last two items in the list.

Contractions

- are formed when two words are joined to make one, shorter word; for example, **It's** is short for **It is** and **won't** is short for **will not**.
- have apostrophes (') in place of the missing letters; for example, in **It's**, the apostrophe takes the place of the **i** in **is**, and in **won't**, it takes the place of the **o** in **not**.

Rule!

The contraction of **will not** is **won't** because it is easier to say than **willn't**.

Another tricky word is **who's**, meaning **'who is'**. Don't confuse it with **whose**; for example, **Who's going to tell me whose hat this is?** **Who's** stands for **Who is** and **whose** means **'who'** it belongs to.

Tip!

Don't confuse **it's** with the possessive pronoun **its**; for example, **It's cold outside, but the dog won't wear its jacket.**

Let's find them!

Apart from **the beach**, **swimming and picnics**, find four more lists in the text.

1 ______________________ 2 ______________________

3 ______________________ 4 ______________________

Find these **contractions** in the text.

5 Summer is ______________________ 6 do not ______________________

7 cannot ______________________

Let's go to the next step!

Underline the lists and put a circle around the **contractions** in these sentences; for example, This spring (we'll) plant <u>red, yellow, purple and pink</u> flowers.

1. This spring we won't be planting lettuce, tomatoes or spinach.
2. In the summer I'm going to swim, play cricket and go to the gym.
3. Gran says she'll knit me a jumper, a scarf and a pair of gloves for the winter.
4. Autumn's the time when the leaves on some trees turn red, gold and orange.
5. This summer we've seen lots of lorikeets, cockatoos and king parrots in our garden.
6. She doesn't know that the order of the seasons is spring, summer, autumn and winter.
7. They're still deciding whether they should go to Brisbane, Adelaide or Perth next summer.

Let's aim high now!

Fill in the missing **commas** and **apostrophes** in th ese sentences; for example:
I dont like winter because its cold wet and miserable.
I don't like winter because it's cold, wet and miserable.

1. I d like to go to Japan in the spring summer or autumn.
2. They ve never been to a spring summer or autumn festival.
3. She doesn t have skis boots or goggles because she hasnt skied before.
4. It isn t as hot in Tasmania as it is in Queensland Victoria or Western Australia.
5. They re predicting that the weather will be cooler wetter and windier this summer.
6. You can t snowboard make snowmen or have snowball fights if it doesnt snow in winter.
7. This autumn we re going to trim the rose bushes tidy the flowerbeds and clean out the shed.

Spring

In my house, spring means it's time to spring clean. This spring, Mum and I started in **my little brother's room** and gradually worked our way through the house. I dusted all **the books' covers** and cleaned out the bird's cage. My older brother helped tidy Dad's shed. He also washed out the dog's kennel. Dad replaced the smoke alarms' batteries, painted the outside doors' frames and cleaned and replaced our bikes' chains. This year he also had to fix the dustbin's lid. Our house is now spick and span!

by Joanne

This is a **recount**. Remember—a recount tells about things that have already happened. Joanne uses **apostrophes** to show ownership while telling what her family did this spring.

In the previous section you learnt that **apostrophes** are used to show missing letters.

Apostrophes are also used to show ownership; for example, **my little brother's room**. The apostrophe shows that the room belongs to Joanne's little brother.

Rule!

- If there is one owner, the apostrophe comes **before** the *s*; for example, **my little brother's room**.
- If there is more than one owner, the apostrophe comes **after** the *s*; for example, **the books' covers**.
- For **irregular plurals** such as **children**, **men** and **people**, the apostrophe always comes **before** the *s*; for example, **the children's sunscreen; the men's hats; the people's beach towels.**

Let's find them!

Find this information in the text. Who or what does the

1. cage belong to? ______________________
2. shed belong to? ______________________
3. kennel belong to? ______________________
4. lid belong to? ______________________

What do the

5. batteries belong to? ______________________
6. frames belong to? ______________________
7. chains belong to? ______________________

Let's go to the next step!

Show who the owners are in these sentences by filling in the **apostrophes**; for example:
In winter we put a heater in our dog's kennel. (one dog)
In winter we put heaters in our dogs' kennels. (more than one dog)

1. The men s job is to clear away the snow.
2. "I have found my sister s sunhat," said Cathy.
3. The children s winter uniforms are in the wash.
4. In spring the city s parks are full of colourful flowers.
5. The sun s rays are stronger in summer than in winter.
6. The students swimming costumes were in their bags.
7. The cars engines were overheating in the hot summer weather.

Tip!
Psst! Read the whole sentence to work it out.

Let's aim high now!

Rewrite these sentences, using **apostrophes** to show ownership; for example:
This book about summer belongs to Roger. This is Roger's book.
These books about summer belong to those boys. These are the boys' books.

1. These winter pyjamas belong to Dad.
   These are ______________________________.
2. This spring garden belongs to my friend.
   This is ______________________________.
3. That thermometer belongs to my teacher.
   That is ______________________________.
4. This beach umbrella belongs to my cousin.
   This is ______________________________.
5. Those snow skis belong to the young men.
   Those are ______________________________.
6. Those autumn crops belong to the farmers.
   Those are ______________________________.
7. These summer clothes belong to the ladies.
   These are ______________________________.

Let's put it together now!

In her description of autumn, this student has left out two **commas**, the apostrophes in three **contractions**, and two **apostrophes** that show ownership. Can you fill them in for her?

I love the colours of autumn, when many trees leaves turn orange red or gold. On our farm its a busy season. We have to harvest crops prepare fields for planting and move many of the animals into barns or sheds. The suns rays arent as strong as in summer, but it isnt cold yet. I like autumn because it is such a mild season.

Let's have fun!

This picture of a winter scene will help you fill in the missing words in the description below. Look for the clues and then fill in the words. Don't forget the **commas** and **apostrophes**.

The snowman is wearing a ________________ ________________ and ________________. He has a carrot for a nose and two black stones for eyes. The little ________________ hair is short, and the two bigger ________________ hair is long. We ________________ see their hair because ________________ hidden by their hoods. The ________________ branches are heavy with snow, and the ________________ ________________ and ________________ seem to be shivering.

Let's have a test!

1 Which sentence has been written correctly?

- ◯ The four seasons are spring, summer, autumn, and winter.
- ◯ The four seasons are spring, summer, autumn and winter.
- ◯ The four seasons are spring summer, autumn and winter.

2 Where should the comma be in this sentence?

In winter I wear a thick ◯ jumper ◯ long ◯ trousers ◯ and warm boots.

3 In which sentence has the contraction been written correctly?

- ◯ Who'se going to summer school?
- ◯ Who's going to summer school?
- ◯ Whos' going to summer school?
- ◯ Wh'os going to summer school?

4 Which words does the contraction replace in this sentence?

He said he'd never known such a cold winter.

◯ he had ◯ he did ◯ he would ◯ he could

Which sentences have been written correctly?

5

- ◯ This little boys' gloves are in his bag.
- ◯ This little boys glove's are in his bag.
- ◯ This little boys gloves' are in his bag.
- ◯ This little boy's gloves are in his bag.

6

- ◯ The child's paintings of autumn are on the wall.
- ◯ The childs' paintings of autumn are on the wall.
- ◯ The childs painting's of autumn are on the wall.
- ◯ The childs paintings' of autumn are on the wall.

Which sentences have been written **incorrectly**?

7

- ◯ The weatherman's predictions were correct.
- ◯ The weathermans' predictions were correct.
- ◯ The weathermen's predictions were correct.

8

- ◯ The goose's feathers keep her warm in the winter.
- ◯ The geese's feathers keep them warm in the winter.
- ◯ The geeses' feathers keep them warm in the winter.

Let's write now!

Choose one of the following activities:

- Write a **poem** about one of the seasons OR
- Write a **description** of one of the seasons.

Try to include lists of **nouns**, **adjectives** or **actions**, **contractions** and **nouns that show ownership** in your poem or description. Don't forget the **commas** and **apostrophes**.

Unit 14 Being adventurous

Focus
Direct and reported speech

Is BMX racing dangerous?

"Mum, why won't you buy me a BMX racing bike for my birthday?" asked Nick.

"I won't let you race on a BMX track," replied Mum, "so it would be a waste of money."

"Oscar and Grant have got BMX bikes," whined Nick. "And you should see the great prizes they win at BMX races!"

"BMX racing is much too dangerous," said Mum.

"Not if you wear the right gear," persisted Nick.

"I've done some research on this, Nick," Mum said calmly. "Wearing the right gear won't stop you from getting injured if you have an accident."

"I promise I'll be careful, Mum," said Nick.

"Humph!" snorted Mum, "you're far too adventurous to be careful! You're not getting a BMX, and that's final!"

This is a type of **discussion**. A discussion looks at both sides of an argument. The author uses **direct speech** to show the exact words Nick and his mum use while discussing the advantages and disadvantages of BMX racing.

Direct speech is quoted speech; for example:

"**Mum, why won't you buy me a BMX racing bike for my birthday?**"

Rule! Always place speech marks around spoken words, including the punctuation mark. In the example sentence, the speech marks come after the question mark.

Let's find them!

Find the missing punctuation marks for these sentences in the text, and then fill them in using a red pen.

1. I won't let you race on a BMX track replied Mum so it would be a waste of money

Tip! A conversation between two or more people is known as **dialogue**.

2. Oscar and Grant have got BMX bikes whined Nick
3. BMX racing is much too dangerous said Mum
4. Not if you wear the right gear persisted Nick
5. I've done some research on this Nick Mum said calmly
6. Wearing the right gear won't stop you from getting injured if you have an accident
7. I promise I'll be careful Mum said Nick

Let's go to the next step!

Underline the spoken words in these sentences; for example,
"I often pretend I'm on an adventure," said Mark.

1. "What an adventure that was!" exclaimed the twins.
2. "How many adventurous things have you done?" asked my friend.
3. "Be adventurous and try something new," commanded the instructor.
4. "Some people are more adventurous than others," explained the man.
5. "The characters in this book have lots of exciting adventures," said Julia.
6. "Jasper is an adventurous boy," said his father, "so I'm sure he'll go on that ride."
7. "Being too adventurous can sometimes get you into trouble," warned my mother.

Let's aim high now!

Underline the spoken words in these sentences and then punctuate them correctly. Remember to add commas, question marks, exclamation marks and full stops, and to place them **inside** the speech marks.

1. One day I'd like to be a skydiver said the boy
2. Vera said My uncle is planning to climb Mount Everest next year
3. I prefer the safe sports to the more adventurous ones said the girl
4. This summer we are going on an outdoor adventure said Lin and Pat
5. What is the most adventurous holiday you have been on asked my teacher
6. Hang gliding jet skiing and rock climbing are extreme sports said Mr Evans
7. Jarred said Scuba diving on the Great Barrier Reef is the most amazing underwater adventure

Paula's trip to Borneo

The travel agent told her that her trip to Borneo would be exciting, and it was! **Paula said she had never seen orangutans in the wild before**. She said it was fantastic to see them in their natural habitat. She warned that visitors to Borneo could expect hot, humid weather, but quickly added that the sweltering heat wouldn't spoil their holiday. She complained that she hadn't had enough time to see all the wonders of Borneo, and declared that she would be returning there in the very near future. She ended by saying that it was the most adventure-filled holiday she had ever been on.

This is a **report**. A report gives us information about people and events. The author uses **reported speech** to tell us what Paula said about her visit to Borneo, without using her exact words.

Reported speech tells what other people said, without using their exact words; for example:

Paula said (that) she had never seen orangutans in the wild before instead of **Paula said, "I have never seen orangutans in the wild before."**

Rule! The verbs in reported speech are written in the past tense; for example:

- She said (that) she wanted a new skateboard.

Let's find them!

Tip! Reported speech does not need speech marks.

Find these examples of **reported speech** in the text. The first one has been done for you.

1. What the travel agent told Paula *Her trip to Borneo would be exciting.*
2. What Paula said about seeing orangutans in their natural habitat ______
3. What Paula warned visitors to Borneo to expect ______
4. What Paula added about the heat ______
5. What Paula complained about ______
6. What Paula declared ______
7. What Paula ended by saying ______

Let's go to the next step!

Write the underlined words in the following sentences in the past tense; for example: He said that he will *would* start taking more risks.

Tip!

Watch out for these verbs!

Present	Past	Present	Past
am	was	are	were
is	was	can	could
will	would	has	had
have	had	do	did

1. Dad said that the new skateboard trick is ______________ too risky.
2. He boasted that he can ______________ do lots of tricks on his bike.
3. She said that she has ______________ been to lots of exciting places.
4. They announced that they are ______________ going to take flying lessons.
5. He said that he finds ______________ out how to do the tricks on the internet.
6. He complained that she takes ______________ too many risks on her scooter.
7. I told them that I am ______________ getting a BMX racing bike for my birthday.

Rule!

When changing direct speech to reported speech, you need to change the **pronouns** as well as the **tense** of the verb; for example:

- "I am going to try that trick," said Kerry.
- Kerry said that she was going to try that trick.

Let's aim high now!

Complete the second sentence in each pair by changing the **pronoun** and the **tense** of the verb; for example,

The girl said, "I don't like watching dangerous sports."

The girl said that she didn't like watching dangerous sports.

1. He said, "I won't try that trick again."
   He said that ______________________ that trick again.
2. "Your helmet isn't in the bag," said Mum.
   Mum said that ______________________ in the bag.
3. The coach said, "You need to take more risks."
   The coach said that ______________________ to take more risks.
4. Jack whispered, "I'm nervous about climbing the wall."
   Jack whispered that ______________________ nervous about climbing the wall.
5. "I hope to go on many adventures one day," said the little boy.
   The little boy said that ______________________ to go on many adventures one day.

6 The skydiver said, “I will try to land in the right spot next time.”

The skydiver said that ______________________________ to land in the right spot next time.

7 “I am going to end the routine with a triple somersault,” declared the gymnast.

The gymnast declared that ______________________________ to end the routine with a triple somersault.

Let’s put it together now!

There are seven mistakes in this student’s work. The words in bold are in the wrong tense; she has left out some speech marks and a comma; and she has used a small letter where she should have used a capital letter. Fill in the missing punctuation and write the correct forms of the verbs in the spaces.

Rick’s dad said he **will** ______________ buy him a skateboard if Rick **promise**

______________ not to try any dangerous tricks.

There’s only one condition, said Rick’s dad. “you can’t go to the skateboard park unless your mum or I are with you.

Rick said it **is** ______________ a deal.

Let’s have fun!

Join Natalie in her challenge by working out what she said on her way up and down the mountain. The first sentence uses direct speech, and the second reported speech.

Find out what Natalie said when she climbed up the mountain by unscrambling these words and punctuation marks. Write the sentence in the space. Make sure you use all the punctuation marks!

hard ! Natalie “ work This . exclaimed , is ”

____

Now find out what Natalie said when she came down the mountain by unscrambling these words and punctuation marks. Write the sentence in the space.

easier Natalie . abseiling said was down that

____

Let's have a test!

Which punctuation marks are missing in these sentences?

1. "He is being very adventurous! exclaimed the spectator.

   ◯ "   ◯ !   ◯ ,   ◯ ?

2. "When are you going hiking again " enquired the man.

   ◯ .   ◯ ,   ◯ ?   ◯ !

Which sentences have been written correctly?

3. ◯ "We're going on an adventure?" Dad announced.
   ◯ "We're going on an adventure!" Dad announced.
   ◯ "We're going on an adventure" Dad announced.
   ◯ "We're going on an adventure." Dad announced.

4. ◯ He said that I am riding my bike too fast.
   ◯ He said that I rides my bike too fast.
   ◯ He said that I was riding my bike too fast.
   ◯ He said that I riding my bike too fast.

Which words should replace the ones in bold in these sentences?

5. The boy said that he **will** be more careful next time.

   ◯ won't   ◯ would   ◯ wouldn't   ◯ must

6. The teacher said that the game they **are** playing **is** too dangerous.

   ◯ was, would   ◯ had, was   ◯ could, was   ◯ were, was

Which sentences have been written **incorrectly**?

7. ◯ "Have you ever been on an adventure trail?" asked the guide.
   ◯ "I've never been on an adventure trail," said the tall man.
   ◯ "We've been on lots of adventure trails," said Janet and John.
   ◯ "I wish I could go on an adventure trail." whined the little girl.

8. ◯ My friend said that it was too risky.
   ◯ My friend said that she thought it was too risky.
   ◯ My friend said that she warned me it would be too risky.
   ◯ My friend said that she warns me it will be too risky.

Let's write now!

Write a **discussion** between two people who have different opinions about an activity like skateboarding, surfing or scootering. One person should argue that the activity is dangerous, while the other person believes it is safe.

Unit 15 What's making news?

Focus
Compound and complex sentences

JELLY KING!

Simon Gillman of Queensland was crowned Jelly-eating King of Australia last night. Simon ate an amazing 2 kilograms of raspberry jelly in less than a minute. When asked how he did it, Simon said, "**Jelly doesn't need chewing, so it was easy**. It just slid down my throat."

Simon won 1000 boxes of jelly and he will be going to the World Jelly-eating Championships. Simon said afterwards, "I might eat all of the jelly myself, or I might share it with my family."

When I asked Simon how he felt after eating all that jelly, he replied, "I feel a bit wobbly, but otherwise I am fine."

The Jelly-eating World Championships take place in New York later this year. We will be cheering for you, Simon!

This is a **newspaper report**. A newspaper report informs readers about important or interesting events. The reporter uses a number of **compound sentences** to tell about the winner of a jelly-eating competition.

In Unit 1 you learned that simple sentences have a subject and a predicate that contains the verb. The subject is the person or thing that does the action, and the predicate is the rest of the sentence; for example, **Simon Gillman of Queensland** (subject) **was crowned Jelly-eating King of Australia last night** (predicate).

- A group of words that contains a subject and a verb is called a clause. A simple sentence has one clause.
- **Compound sentences** are two simple sentences that are joined together to make a single sentence. They have two clauses; for example:
- Jelly doesn't need chewing. It was easy. (two simple sentences)
- **Jelly doesn't need chewing, so it was easy.** (compound sentence)

Words that join simple sentences to make compound sentences are called **conjunctions**.

Let's find them!

Circle the **conjunctions** and underline the **verbs** or **verb groups** in these **compound sentences** from the text.

Tip!

Tip! To make compound sentences, simple sentences are usually joined with the conjunctions **and**, **or**, **but** or **so**.

1. Simon won 1000 boxes of jelly and he will be going to the World Jelly-eating Championships.

2. I might eat all of the jelly myself, or I might share it with my family.
3. I feel a bit wobbly, but otherwise I am fine.

Let's go to the next step!

Are these **simple sentences** or **compound sentences**? Write the answer in the space next to each sentence; for example:

This is an interesting story. **Simple sentence**

This is an interesting story, but that one isn't. **Compound sentence**

1. I have read all of the magazines on the table. ________________
2. I turned on the radio and listened to the news. ________________
3. News about the earthquake is on the front page. ________________
4. He wanted the latest magazine, so I bought it for him. ________________
5. You can read this newspaper, or you can read that one. ________________
6. This is interesting news, but no one has written about it. ________________
7. The main story in today's paper is about global warming. ________________

Let's aim high now!

Choose the correct **conjunction** in brackets to complete these **compound sentences**; for example, I haven't read the story in the newspaper, *but* I have seen it on television. (or, but)

1. The reporter will interview him, ____________ he will interview her. (or, but)
2. The newsreader sat down ____________ started reading the news. (but, and)
3. He wanted to write the report, ____________ he didn't have the time. (but, or)
4. He hasn't seen it on the news, ____________ he knows what happened. (so, but)
5. He didn't watch the early news ____________ he didn't watch the late news. (and, or)
6. I will watch the news on television, ____________ I will listen to it on the radio. (so, or)
7. We were anxious to know what was happening, ____________ we listened to every news bulletin. (or, so)

RAGING ROOSTER

Last week Danh Chu, a 35-year-old farmer from a small village in North Vietnam, came home to find his wife being attacked by their rooster.

Mrs Chu was cowering in a corner of the kitchen while the rooster pecked her feet. The angry bird then turned on Mr Chu when he got too close to it.

Mr Chu eventually got his fishing net, which he threw over the rooster. He was then able to take it outside.

Afterwards Mrs Chu said, "We will have to get rid of the rooster because it no longer likes us." Mrs Chu was so badly shaken by her experience that she is now terrified of all roosters.

The Chus say they will sell the rooster. If no one wants it, they will turn it into chicken noodle soup.

This is another **newspaper report**. The reporter uses a number of **complex sentences** to tell about an angry rooster.

Remember: simple sentences have one clause and make sense on their own.

Compound sentences are two simple sentences joined by a conjunction.

Complex sentences contain a main clause which can stand alone and a subordinate clause. The subordinate clause adds information about the main idea, but cannot stand alone; for example,

Mrs Chu was cowering in a corner of the kitchen (main clause) **while the rooster pecked her feet** (subordinate clause).

Mr Chu eventually got his fishing net (main clause)**, which he threw over the rooster** (subordinate clause)**.**

Subordinate clauses can be joined to the main clause by a conjunction such as **while**, or a pronoun such as **which**.

Rule!

These are some of the conjunctions that join subordinate clauses to main clauses:

after although because if once therefore unless until when while

Pronouns that join subordinate clauses to main clauses are called **relative pronouns**. They are **who, whom, which** and **that**.

Let's find them!

Find the **main clause** and the **subordinate clause** in these **complex sentences** from the text. Underline the main clause and put a box around the subordinate clause.

Tip!

Be careful! The subordinate clause sometimes comes at the beginning of the sentence!

1. The angry bird then turned on Mr Chu when he got too close to it.
2. We will have to get rid of the rooster because it no longer likes us.
3. Mrs Chu was so badly shaken by her experience that she is now terrified of all roosters.
4. If no one wants it, they will turn it into chicken noodle soup.

Let's go to the next step!

Use a **conjunction** or **relative pronoun** from the box to complete these **complex sentences**. Use each word once.

who	that	because	unless	while	until	once

1. I won't buy the magazine __________ you really want it.
2. I will read the newspaper __________ you have finished with it.
3. He always listens to the news __________ he does his homework.
4. The magazine __________ my mother works for won an award this year.
5. I heard the story from a man __________ writes articles for a wildlife magazine.
6. The newspaper will remain in the post box __________ someone brings it inside.
7. I read the newspaper __________ I want to know what is happening in the world.

Let's aim high now!

So far you have learned that a **subordinate clause** can come at the beginning of a sentence or at the end of a sentence. Sometimes, however, it can also come in the middle of a sentence; for example, The newspaper, which is on the table, contains many interesting stories.

The main clause in this sentence is **The newspaper contains many interesting stories** and the subordinate clause is **which is on the table**.

Underline the main clauses and put a box around the subordinate clauses in these sentences.

1. If you write the report, they will publish it.
2. Unless you start immediately, you won't finish the report.
3. Once he has read the magazine, he will give it to his brother.
4. Mum, who is an excellent cook, buys lots of food magazines.

5. George and I will write the story that we discussed yesterday.

6. The article that I read in the newspaper was about global warming.

7. I read the front page first because it contains the most important news.

Let's put it together now!

Can you fill in these **conjunctions** and **relative pronouns** that are missing from this student's report?

if	although	that	but	so	who	because

Scientists at a laboratory in California are training monkeys to perform certain tasks ______________ humans usually do, such as waiting on tables. According to one of the scientists, "Monkeys don't need cash, ______________ they will save their employers money. ______________ people employ monkeys, they can pay them in food."

Some restaurant owners thought that employing monkeys was a good idea, ______________ others weren't so sure. One restaurant owner, ______________ wishes to remain anonymous, said, "Monkeys won't do as good a job as humans ______________ they can't communicate verbally. I definitely won't be using monkeys to wait on my tables, ______________ I know of some restaurant owners who might."

Let's have fun!

Can you unscramble these **conjunctions** and **relative pronouns**?

atth ______________________________

tbu ______________________________

ohw ______________________________

cebusae ______________________________

iwleh ______________________________

neslus ______________________________

cone ______________________________

hicwh ______________________________

Let's have a test!

1 Which of these is a compound sentence?

- ◯ He writes articles for a magazine.
- ◯ He writes articles for a magazine and she edits them.
- ◯ He writes articles for a magazine which is popular with teenagers.
- ◯ I always read the articles that he writes for the magazine.

Which words complete these sentences correctly?

2 He turned on the television, ______________ he didn't watch the news.

◯ so ◯ or ◯ but ◯ if

3 He can sell the extra newspapers, ______________ he can give them away.

◯ but ◯ when ◯ while ◯ or

4 Which sentence has been written correctly?

- ◯ I will read the newspaper and she will read the magazine.
- ◯ I will read the newspaper or she will read the magazine.
- ◯ I will read the newspaper until she will read the magazine.
- ◯ I will read the newspaper after she will read the magazine.

5 Which one is the complex sentence?

- ◯ The story, which was headline news, was in all the newspapers.
- ◯ The story was headline news.
- ◯ The story was in all the newspapers.

Shade the box next to the word that completes each sentence correctly.

6 I will listen to the news ______________ I get home in time.

◯ while ◯ if ◯ therefore ◯ unless

7 This is the magazine ______________ I was telling you about.

◯ who ◯ because ◯ after ◯ that

8 Shade the box next to the sentence that has been written correctly.

- ◯ I heard about the earthquake who destroyed an entire village.
- ◯ I heard about the earthquake that destroyed an entire village.
- ◯ I heard about the earthquake when destroyed an entire village.

Let's write now!

Think of something interesting that has happened at school and write a **report** about it for your school newsletter. Try to use a mixture of **simple**, **compound** and **complex sentences**.

Unit 16 Secrets of the sea

Focus

Punctuating sentences; quotation marks

The coral reef

After I had completed my scuba diving course, Mum and Dad bought me an underwater camera. **Dad asked one of his friends, an experienced scuba diver, to take me with him on his next dive**. I was excited, but I was also a bit nervous. What if something went wrong with my equipment? What if I came face to face with a shark? I eventually convinced myself that that was unlikely to happen. In any case, Dad's friend Jim had been diving for years and nothing bad had ever happened to him.

The day of the dive finally arrived, with not a cloud in the sky. Jim got to our house early and helped me get my gear together. **When everything was ready, I waved goodbye to Mum and Dad and off we set.** By this time, the butterflies in my stomach were doing a war dance! I wanted to tell Jim how nervous I was, but I also didn't want him to think I was a coward.

This is the opening paragraph of a **narrative**. The author uses **commas** to create pauses and make the text easier to understand.

In Unit 13 you learnt that commas are used to separate items in a list, and in Unit 14 you learnt how to use commas when writing dialogue.

You have also learnt in Units 11 and 15 about phrases and subordinate clauses adding extra detail to sentences.

Commas are also used to separate phrases and clauses from the rest of the sentence, helping to make the meaning clear.

In the following sentence, commas are used to separate the phrase **an experienced scuba diver** from the rest of the sentence.

Dad asked one of his friends, an experienced scuba diver, to take me with him on his next dive.

In the next sentence, a comma is used to separate the subordinate clause **when everything was ready** from the rest of the sentence.

When everything was ready, I waved goodbye to Mum and Dad and off we set.

Let's find them!

Find these sentences in the text and fill in the missing **commas**.

1. After I had completed my scuba diving course Mum and Dad bought me an underwater camera.
2. I was excited but I was also a bit nervous.
3. In any case Dad's friend Jim had been diving for years and nothing bad had ever happened to him.
4. The day of the dive finally arrived with not a cloud in the sky.
5. By this time the butterflies in my stomach were doing a war dance!

Tip!

Tip! When joining two **main clauses** to form a **compound sentence**, there is usually a comma before the conjunction **but**; for example, **I wanted to tell Jim how nervous I was, but I also didn't want him to think I was a coward.**

Let's go to the next step!

In the sentences below, use **commas** to separate the **phrases** from the rest of the sentence. If you're not sure, read the sentence out loud and work out where you might pause slightly. That's where the comma should be!

1. On a scale from one to ten I'd say that dive was worth a ten!
2. Some sharks especially the very big ones are truly terrifying.
3. To my great surprise we saw more sea horses than clownfish.
4. At that moment a huge octopus appeared from behind the rock.
5. By the way those photographs you took of the coral reef are outstanding.
6. The fish one of the most beautiful of its kind was hiding amongst the coral.
7. Without a doubt that was the most exciting underwater experience I've ever had.

Let's aim high now!

Now use **commas** to separate the **clauses** in these sentences. Remember: if you're not sure, read the sentence out loud and listen for the pauses.

1. If you spend too long underwater you'll start to feel sick.
2. The fish which is highly poisonous looks just like a rock.
3. We saw lots of beautiful fish but we also saw some ugly ones.
4. From where we were sitting we could just see the wrecked ship.
5. While I was photographing the reef a sea snake swam right in front of me.
6. Because I'd never seen a sea dragon before I didn't know what I was looking for.
7. The boy who everyone thought was an experienced diver got into trouble underwater.

Waves of Fear

The sea fascinates me. I have watched dozens of movies and documentaries about life underwater, from 'The Little Mermaid' to **'The Blue Planet'**. I have read books that tell of amazing adventures at sea, like 'Treasure Island', 'Robinson Crusoe' and 'Twenty Thousand Leagues Under the Sea'. The DVDs that I watch over and over again are 'Finding Nemo', 'Shark Tale' and 'Free Willy', and my favourite song is **'Under the Sea'**. You might think that I love going to the beach and being in the water. Wrong! When my family forces me to go with them to the beach, I stay as far away from those waves as I can!

This is another opening paragraph of a **narrative**. The author uses **quotation marks** and **capital letters** to indicate the titles of films, TV programs, books and a song, while telling of her fear of the water.

Quotation marks are used around the titles of books, films, plays, poems, TV programs, magazines and songs; for example, **'The Blue Planet'**. In typed text, italics may be used instead of quotation marks; for example, ***The Blue Planet***.

Rule! The first letter of each word in the title of a book, film, TV program, magazine or song starts with a **capital letter**. The exceptions are little words like **a**, **an**, **the**, **in**, **and**, **of** and **for**, which start with a small letter, unless they come at the beginning of the title; for example, **'Under the Sea'**.

Let's find them!

Apart from 'The Blue Planet', find the titles of seven films, TV programs, books or DVDs in the text and write them in the spaces. Don't forget to put **quotation marks** around them.

1 ______________________
2 ______________________
3 ______________________
4 ______________________
5 ______________________
6 ______________________
7 ______________________

Tip! If there is a punctuation mark **after** the title, it comes after the quotation mark; for example, **My favourite song is 'Under the Sea'.**

Let's go to the next step!

Put **quotation marks** around the titles of radio and TV programs, books and magazines in these sentences. Remember to place any **punctuation** marks that come after the title **after** the quotation mark.

1. My favourite TV program is Underwater Adventure .
2. The Diver is a magazine that comes out once a month .
3. My father has written a book called A Guide to Underwater Photography .
4. Jessica Watson's book about her experiences at sea is called True Spirit .
5. I heard about the fishing competition on the radio program, Catch of the Day .
6. She found information about the tides and weather in the magazine, Surf's Up .
7. The young sailor was interviewed on the breakfast show, Good Morning, America .

Let's aim high now!

Use a red pen to circle the letters that should be **capitalised** in the titles in these sentences.

1. My brother's favourite film is 'pirates of the caribbean'.
2. A famous poem about the sea is 'the rime of the ancient mariner'.
3. My father is working on a documentary called 'tales of a deep sea diver'.
4. Mum found a recipe for an unusual fish pie in the new edition of 'what's for dinner?'.
5. My little sister's new library book is called 'five little sharks swimming in the sea'.
6. Our music teacher has written a song called 'pretty little seashells' for the school play.
7. The Australian television series, 'H2O: just add water', is filmed at Sea World on the Gold Coast.

Let's put it together now!

This student has left out **commas**, **quotation marks** and **capital letters** in this opening paragraph of a narrative. Use a red pen to make the corrections.

The afternoon started well. Mum was stretched out on a deck chair, reading the latest copy of The Australian Woman's Weekly ; Dad was waiting patiently for a fish to bite; Jackie was playing 'popping penguins' on Mum's phone, and I was slowly drifting off to sleep, lulled by the gentle movement of the boat. Then it happened. A squall which seemed to come out of nowhere whipped Mum's magazine right out of her hands. Jackie who was sitting beside me looked up in alarm. Dad told us not to worry but I could see that he was nervous. That's when I felt the panic rise inside me.

Let's have fun!

Draw lines to match these titles to their descriptions. Do the obvious ones first, and then work out the more difficult ones.

Title		Description
'Mermaids and Mermen: Myth or Reality?'		A magazine for fishermen
'Riding the Waves'		A TV documentary about ships that carry passengers
'Giants of the Deep'		A cartoon for young children
'The Ballad of the Sea'		A TV program about the biggest animals in the sea
'Hook, Line and Sinker'		A book that questions whether certain sea creatures really exist
'Treasures on the Ocean Floor'		An adventure story about a group of children who get shipwrecked on a desert island
'Luxury Liners'		A poem about the sea
'Flippy and Flynn Go to Sea'		A story about pirates
'Captain Blackbeard Meets His Match'		A TV program about old shipwrecks
'Coconut Island'		A magazine for surfers

Let's have a test!

Which sentence has been written correctly?

1
- ○ In the olden days people didn't know much about the oceans.
- ○ In the olden days, people didn't know much, about the oceans.
- ○ In the olden days people didn't know much, about the oceans.
- ○ In the olden days, people didn't know much about the oceans.

Which words and punctuation complete these sentences correctly?

2 If I go diving ______________________ will take more photographs.

- ○ , again I
- ○ again. I
- ○ again, I
- ○ again I,

3 I haven't been ______________________ I haven't seen any whales.

- ○ sailing yet, so
- ○ sailing, yet so
- ○ sailing yet. So
- ○ sailing yet so,

Where should the missing commas go?

4 I have never ○ seen a killer whale ○ but ○ I know ○ what it looks like.

5 The fish ○ which ○ is extremely rare ○ is on show ○ at the aquarium.

Where should the missing quotation marks go?

6 His new book is called ○ The ○ Call of the Sea ○ ○ .

7 His new documentary, ○ Predators of the Deep ○ , ○ is popular with viewers ○ .

8 Which choice completes the sentence correctly?

The song that introduces the documentary is called ______________________.

- ○ 'Shark Attack'.
- ○ 'Shark Attack.
- ○ 'Shark Attack?
- ○ 'Shark Attack'

Let's write now!

Write a **narrative** that has something to do with the sea. Use a mixture of **simple**, **compound** and **complex sentences**. Make sure you punctuate your sentences correctly.

Glossary of terms

Adjectives describe nouns and pronouns. Types of adjectives are:
- **comparing adjectives**, e.g. quieter, quietest
- **descriptive adjectives**, e.g. short, round, little, friendly
- **number adjectives**, e.g. some, many, four.

Adverbs add meaning to verbs by telling how, where or when something is done, e.g. quickly, outside, yesterday.

Antonyms are words that are opposite in meaning, e.g. happy—sad.

Apostrophes are punctuation marks that show:
- where letters are missing in words, e.g. they're (they are)
- ownership, e.g. Jo's book (the book belonging to Jo).

Articles are the words **a**, **an** and **the**.

Clauses are groups of words that express a complete thought and contain a verb or verb group.

Commands are sentences that tell someone to do something. They usually end with a full stop (.) or sometimes an exclamation mark (!).

Commas (,) are punctuation marks that separate items in a list or separate phrases and clauses from the rest of the sentence.

Conjunctions connect words, phrases and clauses in sentences, e.g. and, but, or.

Contractions are words formed when two words are joined to make one, shorter word, e.g. don't (do not).

Exclamations are sentences that express strong feelings. They end with an exclamation mark (!).

Nouns are naming words. There are several types of nouns:
- **Abstract nouns** name ideas and feelings, e.g. darkness, happiness.
- **Collective nouns** name groups of people, animals, places or things, e.g. herd, flock.
- **Common nouns** name general people, animals, places or things, e.g. girl, dog, country, car.
- **Compound nouns** are formed by joining two or more words together, e.g. sunlight.
- **Proper nouns** name specific people, animals, places or things, e.g. Tom, Rover, Australia, Halloween.
- **Singular** and **plural nouns**, e.g. book → books.

Phrases are groups of words that do not make sense on their own. Usually they don't contain a verb, e.g. in the city, with long hair.

Prepositions are words that connect nouns, pronouns and phrases with other words in a sentence by telling where and when, e.g. in, on, from, since, until.

Pronouns are words that are used in place of nouns. These are:
- personal **pronouns**, e.g. he, she
- possessive **pronouns**, e.g. his, her.

Questions are sentences that ask for information or opinions. They always end with a question mark (?).

Quotation marks are punctuation marks (' ') that are placed around titles of books, songs, TV programs, etc.

Reported speech tells what other people said, without using their exact words, e.g. He said that he would try to help us.

Sentences are groups of words that make sense on their own. They always start with a capital letter and can end with a full stop, question mark or exclamation mark.

- **Simple sentences** contain only one verb.
- **Compound sentences** are two simple sentences that are joined together by a conjunction to form a single sentence.
- **Complex sentences** consist of a main clause and one or more subordinate clauses.

Speech marks are punctuation marks (“ ”) that are placed around spoken language.

Statements are sentences that give information or opinions. They always start with a capital letter and end with a full stop.

Subjects are the people, animals or things in a sentence that do the action.

Suffixes are groups of letters attached to the ends of words to change their meaning, e.g. bright, brighter, brightness, brightly.

Tense shows when an action takes place— **present**, **past** or **future**, e.g. walk, walked, will walk.

Verbs are words that show what people, animals or things do. Types of verbs are:

- **being** and **having verbs**, e.g. is, was, has, had
- **doing verbs**, e.g. run
- **helping verbs**, e.g. can, will
- **saying** and **thinking verbs**, e.g. whispered, thought.

Answers

Unit 1 School excursions

Let's find them! (page 1)

1 A guide showed **us around**.
2 Another machine divided **the mixture into portions**.
3 The freshly baked loaves smelled **delicious**!
4 A conveyor carried **the loaves to the slicing machine**.
5 The best part of our visit came **right at the end**.
6 We each got **a piece of dough**.
7 It tasted **amazing**!

Let's go to the next step! (page 2)

1 Our next excursion will be to the Botanic Gardens.
2 Lots of schools were visiting the museum that day.
3 We went on an excursion to the art gallery last term.
4 Our teachers arrange lots of excursions for us every year.
5 One of my favourite places for a school excursion is the beach.
6 A man at the museum gave us directions to the dinosaur exhibit.
7 School excursions are fun for the students, but not always for the teachers.

Let's aim high now! (page 2)

1 We saw lots of interesting animals at the zoo.
2 Every year thousands of students visit the zoo.
3 Some excursions are more interesting than others.
4 We had to write a recount about our visit to the zoo.
5 The bus dropped the children right in front of the museum.
6 My friends and I ate our lunch near the giraffes' enclosure.
7 The education officer told us about the zoo's education program.

Let's find them! (page 3)

1 went 2 was 3 showed 4 are 5 came 6 caught 7 died

Let's go to the next step! (page 4)

1 I
2 My worksheet
3 A large bird
4 The bus driver
5 Our teacher
6 The Year 6s
7 The little boy

Let's aim high now! (page 4)

1 Our class went on a tour of the art gallery.
2 The lady at the observatory let us look through a telescope.
3 The bus driver took us to the wrong place.
4 Our guide at the museum told us where the fossils were from.
5 The visit to the CSIRO has been my favourite excursion so far.
6 The people at the CSIRO taught us about energy and movement.
7 Those students have been on three excursions this year.

Let's put it together now! (page 5)

Last week the Year 3s and 4s went to a studio. An orchestra played music for us. The conductor told us about the different instruments. He asked us lots of questions. One of my friends conducted the orchestra. He did a good job. The conductor congratulated him afterwards.

Let's have fun! (page 5)

My friend sat next to me on the bus.
The baker gave us each a bun.
One of the musicians showed us a trombone.
Our teachers got us into line.
A kind lady showed us around the museum.

Let's have a test! (page 6)

1 Our class went to the aquarium to see the dugongs.
2 in a glass cabinet at the museum
3 The whole class enjoyed the play.

4 We to the art gallery last week.
5 The fish
6 The curtains
7 are the chimpanzees.
8 often us on excursions.

Unit 2 So that's how it works!

Let's find them! (page 7)

1 It hovered above the paddock for a minute or two, **and then slowly descended**.
2 It looked like **a wide-brimmed silver hat on legs**.
3 Suddenly **he stopped**.
4 Immediately, part of the surface slid aside, **creating an entry into the craft**.
5 How are **you going to do that**?
6 Have you **found something**?
7 What do you think **this is for**?

Let's go to the next step! (page 8)

1 He used a trolley to move that object.
2 Which machine would you rather buy?
3 Why do furniture removers use ramps?
4 Do you know that a ramp is a useful tool?
5 Some tools make a gardener's job easier.
6 How many machines are there in his shed?
7 I would dig the hole with that shovel over there.

Let's aim high now! (page 8)

Questions	Statements
1 How do I unlock this door?	You could try turning the key.
2 What sets a bicycle in motion?	It'll move if someone pushes or pedals it.
3 How can I turn this water into ice?	I suggest you put it in the freezer.
4 What is the purpose of a machine?	It makes work easier.
5 Will he be able to get onto the roof?	Yes, he has a ladder.
6 Can you help me get this nail into the wood?	You can use my hammer.
7 How are goods transported around the country?	They are carried in large trucks.

Let's find them! (page 9)

1 Exclamation
2 Exclamation
3 Command
4 Exclamation
5 Command
6 Command
7 Command

Let's go to the next step! (page 10)

1 Use scissors.
2 Undo the clasps.
3 What a brilliant invention!
4 Put the wheels on the cart.
5 How amazing is that machine!
6 I can't believe my invention works!
7 Show your sister how to tie her shoelaces.

Let's aim high now! (page 10)

1 <u>What</u> a fantastic tool this is!
2 <u>Push</u> the trolley and it will start moving.
3 <u>This</u> is the best scooter that was ever invented!
4 <u>How</u> amazing that such a large machine can fly!
5 <u>Attach</u> a handle to the brush to turn it into a broom.
6 <u>Place/Slip</u> a wedge under the door to stop it from slamming.
7 <u>Place/Slip</u> a rope around the wheel and then see if your pulley works.

Let's put it together now! (page 11)

"How does it work? There must be some way to get it started," said Matt. Chen flicked the switch on and off again. This time it did work. The little red car sped across the room and crashed into the wall. The boys looked at each other.

"That was awesome!" exclaimed Rob. "Link it up to the computer, Matt, and let's try to control it this time. Do you need the instructions?" Matt shook his head. He'd gone over it so many times in his head, he knew exactly what to do.

"We've done it, guys!" exclaimed Chen. "We've finally done it!"

Let's have fun! (page 11)

Would you like to know my secret?
Tickle a part of my body.
It's either my chin or the tip of my nose.
It's his chin!
Tickle the monkey's chin to make him laugh.

Let's have a test! (page 12)

1 This is a pulley.
2 Place the rolling pin on the table.
3 ?
4 Do you know how your new computer works!
5 Put more staples in the stapler.
6 Insert
7 !
8 So that's how it works!

Unit 3 Endangered animals

Let's find them! (page 13)

1 squirrels 2 stripes 3 termites 4 tongues 5 settlers 6 foxes 7 cats/dogs

Let's go to the next step! (page 14)

1 This rare parrot is an endangered bird.
2 We saw two big pandas when we went to the zoo.
3 Some elephants in certain countries are endangered.
4 There are many reptiles on the list of endangered animals.
5 This particular possum has large front teeth for cracking nuts.
6 Turtles that live in swamps feed on tadpoles, shrimps and worms.
7 Many endangered marsupials feed on the gum and sap of eucalyptus trees.

Let's aim high now! (page 14)

1 cave 2 penguin 3 tag 4 ocean 5 Tigers 6 scientist 7 students

Let's find them! (page 15–16)

1 Brad 2 Africa/Australia 3 Vanuatu 4 Shark Bay 5 Western Australia 6 December 7 Australia

Let's go to the next step! (page 16)

1 My dog Waggles is not an endangered animal!
2 My parents donate money to the World Wildlife Fund.
3 The last thylacine died in Hobart Zoo in September 1936.
4 The pandas at Adelaide Zoo are called Wang Wang and Funi.
5 On Tuesday we went whale watching in a boat called Sandpiper.
6 Some endangered animals live in the Blue Mountains in New South Wales.
7 A type of frog that lives near the Murray River could become extinct one day.

Let's aim high now! (page 16)

1 England 2 Colo 3 July 4 Mr Stevens 5 Miss Swann 6 Melbourne Zoo 7 Wildlife Conservation Society

Let's put it together now! (page 17)

This little **lizard** is found in the Mount **Lofty** Ranges near **Adelaide** in South Australia. There are fewer than 6000 of these little reptiles left in **Australia**. The main reason they are dying out is that their **habitat** is being destroyed. The lizards find safety in spider **holes**, so in areas where there are more spider holes, there are more of these little **reptiles**.

Let's have fun! (page 17)

d	u	g	o	n	g		A			
				u			f			
D	e	c	e	m	b	e	r			c
				b			i			a
I	n	d	i	a	n		c			t
				t		t	a	i	l	s
						e				
			S	h	a	r	k			
				u		m				
				m		i				
			s	a	l	t				
				n		e				
				s	i	s	t	e	r	

Let's have a test! (page 18)

1 animal 2 place 3 person 4 We saw lots of endangered birds at the bird park. 5 person 6 thing 7 place 8 In April we are going to Queensland to see a rare reptile.

Unit 4 Tales from long ago

Let's find them! (page 19–20)

1 hordes **2** pack **3** troop **4** herd **5** sunrise **6** sunset **7** fireflies

Let's go to the next step! (page 20)

1. Jody is the best storyteller in our class.
2. My grandmother told me a tale about a gang of thieves.
3. In the story, a plague of locusts invades the countryside.
4. Today we read a story about a woodcutter who lived in a forest.
5. This tale is about a colony of bats that turns into humans at daybreak.
6. I listened to the collection of stories while sitting in my favourite armchair.
7. The scariest story in the book is about a criminal mastermind who has his own army.

Let's aim high now! (page 20)

Collective nouns: crowd, bouquet, heap, cluster, tribe, litter, batch

Compound nouns: full moon, fairy tale, son-in-law, housework, chopsticks, toadstool, rainbow

Let's find them! (page 21)

1 peacefulness **2** coolness **3** fear **4** bravery **5** darkness **6** brightness **7** happiness

Let's go to the next step! (page 22)

1. The prince was dazzled by the brilliance of her smile.
2. In the story, the people were punished for their greed.
3. The prince showed great courage in overcoming the dragon.
4. Many stories teach us the importance of being kind to others.
5. The wizard's wickedness was well known throughout the land.
6. The children were filled with wonder when they heard the story.
7. The story is about a poor man who is rewarded for his generosity.

Let's aim high now! (page 22)

2. Showing great loyalty, the king's servants remained with him.
3. Using his imagination, the inventor made two pairs of wings.
4. With a feeling of pride, the queen watched her son receive his prize.
5. In a moment of uncertainty, the prince looked to his father for guidance.
6. With a burst of speed, the hare raced towards the finishing line.
7. To celebrate their victory, the king announced that the next day would be a holiday.
8. As a mark of their friendship, the two girls gave each other a special gift.

Let's put it together now! (page 23)

A folktale from India

A swan with golden feathers once tried to help a poor **family**. It gave them one feather a day to sell at the **marketplace**. But then the mother was filled with **greed**. She told her children to help her pluck all the swan's feathers. As they held the golden feathers, they watched in **horror** as they turned into chicken feathers! The swan was filled with **sadness** and hid amongst the reeds. Before the first **snowfall**, she joined another **flock** and flew away.

Let's have fun! (page 23)

1. a howl of wolves, a flame of dragons, a slice of swords
2.

t	a	e	b	t	r	a	e	h	c	z	r
t	u	x	p	k	b	x	d	a	h	m	e
w	h	o	u	s	e	w	o	r	k	n	h
s	t	y	w	f	n	m	z	e	f	g	t
c	v	g	a	h	m	f	w	q	d	h	o
n	d	q	m	o	l	f	x	z	o	u	m
m	r	o	w	k	l	i	s	h	w	k	d
c	u	g	h	j	s	y	j	s	n	s	n
b	f	g	s	h	a	f	h	c	p	a	a
w	c	h	o	m	q	g	w	J	o	p	r
z	d	w	j	k	s	u	n	L	u	d	g
y	h	y	h	s	h	e	t	n	r	m	w

3. How frightening!—fear
Well done!—congratulations
I don't believe it!—shock
Thank goodness that's over!—relief
Thank you so much!—gratitude
I'm enjoying this!—fun
I always do as I'm told.—obedience

Let's have a test! (page 24)

1. army
2. bundle
3. When the princess cried, her teardrops turned into diamonds.

4 monsters
5 courage
6 opportunity
7 This folktale has a lot of humour in it.
8 The kind man was always prepared to help others.

Unit 5 Pirates

Let's find them! (page 25–26)

1 heroes **2** ships **3** pistols **4** topazes **5** dishes **6** weapons **7** matches

Let's go to the next step! (page 26)

galleons	ropes
masts	rashes
sashes	taxes
crosses	beaches
catches	potatoes
moustaches	mosquitoes
crashes	cameos

Let's aim high now! (page 26)

1 rushes **2** bunches **3** seas **4** chests **5** foxes **6** calicoes **7** tornadoes

Let's find them! (page 27)

1 women **2** ladies **3** scarves **4** lives **5** trousers **6** silver **7** rubies

Let's go to the next step! (page 28)

duties	selves
skies	reefs
countries	halves
armies	dwarves/dwarfs
parties	measles
spies	children
cries	equipment

Let's aim high now! (page 28)

2 bread **3** thieves **4** shelves **5** bullies **6** babies **7** cliffs **8** furniture

Let's put it together now! (page 29)

injuries
mice
cockroaches
tomatoes
animals
calves
sheep

Let's have fun! (page 29)

skulls
trees
axes
mangoes
butterflies
wolves
geese
salmon

Let's have a test! (page 30)

1 Pirates stored their food in barreles.
2 The injured pirate had to use crutchs.
3 In the days of the pirates, there were no radioes.
4 The pirate had two canarys.
5 Some pirates had wifes.
6 Some pirates had bare foots.
7 grandfathers, grandmothers and grandchilds
8 bandanas, eye patches, hats

Unit 6 Healthy living

Let's find them! (page 31–32)

he	she
herself	they
them	you
him	her
us	yourself
himself	

Let's go to the next step! (page 32)

1 herself **2** themselves **3** yourself **4** himself **5** ourselves **6** myself **7** yourselves

Let's aim high now! (page 32)

2 Ginny **3** Advertisements **4** The mother **5** Julie and Jake **6** Veronica **7** The child **8** the children

Let's find them! (page 33–34)

his
Whose
her
hers
their
my
yours
our
your
What

Let's go to the next step! (page 34)

2 the dog **3** Uncle Joe **4** Zack **5** Ken and Kathy **6** apple **7** Mia and Casey **8** Jordan

Let's aim high now! (page 34)

2 Who **3** yours **4** mine **5** theirs **6** Which **7** hers **8** ours

Let's put it together now! (page 35)

Give you health a boost with ours delicious, nutritious Rocket Punch!
Us have used only the freshest fruit, vegetables and herbs to make this amazing drink. Come and try it for yourselves. It strong flavour will knock your socks off! Buy some for your friends and family. Them will love you for introducing they to this wonder drink!

your
our
We
yourselves
Its
They
them

Let's have fun! (page 35)

health—he
nourish—our
cherry—he/her
asparagus—us
wholemeal—who/me
sweet potato—we
cashew—she/he
fitter—it

Let's have a test! (page 36)

1 Would you like to come with us to the gym?
2 They made the salad themselves.
3 us
4 himself
5 My cereal is healthier than yours.
6 Who is the fittest person in the class?
7 their
8 Which

Unit 7 Wonders of the world

Let's find them! (page 37)

1 square **2** white **3** tall **4** spectacular **5** large **6** colourful **7** still

Let's go to the next step! (page 38)

ancient—modern
first—last
beautiful—ugly
many—few
top—bottom
bright—dull
wide—narrow
smooth—rough
present—past
hard—soft
dangerous—safe
deep—shallow
huge—tiny

Let's aim high now! (page 38)

1 peaceful **2** comfortable **3** helpful **4** careless **5** drinkable **6** knowledgeable **7** useless

Let's find them! (page 39–40)

1 most interesting **2** largest **3** wider **4** easier **5** more difficult **6** taller **7** more important

Let's go to the next step! (page 40)

Adjective	Comparing two	Comparing more than two	Adjective	Comparing two	Comparing more than two
big	bigger	biggest	amazing	more amazing	most amazing
pretty	prettier	prettiest	wonderful	more wonderful	most wonderful
fantastic	more fantastic	most fantastic	long	longer	longest
crowded	more crowded	most crowded	enormous	more enormous	most enormous
shady	shadier	shadiest	steep	steeper	steepest
magnificent	more magnificent	most magnificent	great	greater	greatest
heavy	heavier	heaviest	stunning	more stunning	most stunning

Let's aim high now! (page 40)

1 older **2** hottest **3** most beautiful **4** best **5** more enjoyable **6** more interesting **7** more tiring

Let's put it together now! (page 41)

Of the seven wonders of the ancientest world, the Great Pyramid of Giza is the oldest. Some people think it is also the spectacularest. It was the taller building in the world until 700 years ago. Because it is a pyramid, it gets narrower and narrowest as it gets towards the top. The south side of the pyramid is the long of the four sides, and the north side is the shorter. The difference in the length of the two sides is only about 15 cm. There are two main chambers inside the pyramid—the King's Chamber and the Queen's Chamber. The King's Chamber is the biggest of the two.

ancient
most spectacular
tallest
narrower
longest
shortest
bigger

Let's have fun! (page 41)

snake	safe	spider	landslide	thorns	trap	soldiers
spear	refreshing	mosquito	storm	ants	darkness	floods
scorpion	greener	brilliant	cliff	quicksand	thirst	mud
waterfall	vulture	cool	tired	excited	heat	ravine
fire	animals	rocks	accident	special	hunger	mountain

Let's have a test! (page 42)

1. more
2. many
3. obedient
4. magnificent, friendly
5. more beautiful
6. worst
7. The valuablest treasure came from this chamber.
8. The tunnel we went down was widest than theirs.

Unit 8 The magical world of animation

Let's find them! (page 43–44)

1 chooses **2** fight **3** discovers **4** learns **5** rewarded **6** happens **7** watch

Let's go to the next step! (page 44)

1. I laughed all the way through the film.
2. I always buy my cinema tickets online.
3. Sometimes I cry when I watch a sad film.
4. They open the cinema doors at 10 o'clock.
5. We waited in a long queue at the ticket office.
6. I went to the cinema to see the new animated film.
7. The boy who sat next to me in the cinema spilled his popcorn.

Let's aim high now! (page 44)

1. I **walked** up the aisle towards my seat.
2. Not everyone **likes** animated films.
3. At the end of the film, the prince **marries** the princess.
4. Today our teacher **told** us how they **create** animated films.
5. I **gave** my friend some of my chocolates before the film **started**.
6. People in the audience **screamed** when they **saw** the monster.
7. My baby sister **giggled** when the penguins **waddled** onto the screen.

Let's find them! (page 45)

1 have **2** are **3** must **4** is **5** can **6** will **7** should

Let's go to the next step! (page 46)

1. I will go with you to see the new animated film.
2. You can watch the film, but it may upset you.
3. He is sitting next to my brother in the back row.
4. My friend was watching *Shrek* when I went to visit her.
5. You really must see that animated film about penguins.
6. I am looking forward to going to the cinema with you tomorrow.
7. I could tell you how the film ends, but that would spoil it for you.

Let's aim high now! (page 46)

1 will watch **2** has been **3** were waiting **4** have seen **5** will let **6** should go **7** must take

Let's put it together now! (page 47)

One of my favourite animated films is *Finding Nemo*. It is about a little clownfish called Nemo, who lives with his father on the Great Barrier Reef. One day, a scuba diver captures Nemo. Nemo ends up in a small aquarium in a dentist's room. While his father and a fish called Dory are looking everywhere for him, Nemo tries to escape.

If you have not watched this film, I recommend that you do. I don't think it will spoil it for you if I tell you that it has a happy ending.

Let's have fun! (page 47)

					w	o	u	l	d
	h				i				
	a				l				
	s	h	o	u	l	d			
		a				i			
c		v				d			
a	r	e							
n									

Let's have a test! (page 48)

1 listen **2** borrow **3** writes **4** sent **5** does **6** would **7** They might go to the cinema once a week. **8** She tried to make her own animated film.

Unit 9 Festivals and holidays

Let's find them! (page 49)

1 announced **2** told/tell **3** screams **4** think **5** reckons **6** hope **7** love

Let's go to the next step! (page 50)

1 I like dressing up for Halloween.
2 I wonder if we'll go trick-or-treating this year.
3 It annoys me when people don't behave at festivals.
4 We all gasped when they threw the acrobat into the air.
5 Everyone remarked on how beautiful the floats were this year.
6 People cheered when the festival queen walked onto the stage.
7 I guessed how many lollies there were in the jar and won an iPod.

Let's aim high now! (page 50)

1 I **discussed** the arrangements for my party with my mum. **Saying verb**
2 It **fascinates** me to see how other people celebrate Christmas. **Feeling verb**
3 The man next to me **grumbled** that he couldn't see the stage. **Saying verb**
4 Do you **remember** what you got for your birthday last year? **Thinking verb**
5 I **shouted** for joy when our team won the dragon boat race. **Saying verb**
6 I **imagine** there must be many different ways of celebrating the arrival of spring. **Thinking verb**
7 It **irritates** me when he boasts about all the lollies he got for Halloween. **Feeling verb**

Let's find them! (page 51–52)

1 was **2** is **3** had **4** were **5** has been **6** has **7** are **8** will be

Let's go to the next step! (page 52)

1 We will be in Korea for the New Year celebrations.
2 I have been to the Lotus Lantern Festival in Korea.
3 I am at the stadium where the parade will take place.
4 There were lots of people in the park on Children's Day.
5 There are lots of festivals in the world that I don't know about.
6 It has been fun to see the different costumes people wear at festivals.
7 I have pleasant memories of spending Children's Day with Joon's family.

Let's aim high now! (page 52)

1 is **2** been **3** has **4** was **5** be **6** were **7** are

Let's put it together now! (page 53)

Ireland **is** great, and so **are** Dad's Irish relatives. We're staying with them for a few days. Yesterday **was** St Patrick's Day. Aunt Maud took us into town to watch the St Patrick's Day Parade. Shaun **thought** it was boring, but I **enjoyed** it. Most of the people were wearing something green, especially bunches of shamrocks. Aunt Maud **explained** that the shamrock is the symbol of Ireland. Some of the people in the parade **had** on green leprechaun suits. They looked hilarious.

Let's have fun! (page 53)

'Being' verbs: was been are
'Having' verbs: have has had
Saying verbs: complain mutter stated
Thinking verbs: understand remind decide
Feeling verbs: sadden upsets angers

Let's have a test! (page 54)

1 He replied that he had watched the parade.
2 I sometimes wonder if I will ever go to a snow festival.
3 She cheered up when the parade started.
4 warned
5 frighten
6 were
7 Some of the marchers had bagpipes.
8 been

Unit 10 Exploring the unknown

Let's find them! (page 55–56)

1 thought 2 was 3 sailed 4 started 5 were sailing 6 reached 7 arrived

Let's go to the next step! (page 56)

1 Many explorers died in foreign lands.
2 The early explorers spent many months at sea.
3 Captain Cook's ship scraped the Great Barrier Reef.
4 Some European countries were hoping to find new lands.
5 Many people think that the early explorers were very brave men.
6 The explorer was crossing the Antarctic Circle when he saw the iceberg.
7 James Cook mapped the New Zealand and eastern Australian coastlines in 1870.

Let's aim high now! (page 56)

1 Christopher Columbus **went** to America four times.
2 Many early explorers **were** afraid of sailing into the unknown.
3 Matthew Flinders **was** the first man to sail right around Australia.
4 Some early explorers in Australia **disappeared** without trace.
5 Charles Sturt **journeyed** to northern New South Wales at the beginning of the 19th century.
6 Gregory Blaxland, William Lawson and William Wentworth **found** a way across the Blue Mountains.
7 While some settlers **were making** attempts to reach the interior of Australia, others **were settling** around the coast.

Let's find them! (page 57)

1 will be 2 are going to leave 3 will pass 4 will reach 5 will happen 6 will wander 7 will learn

Let's go to the next step! (page 58)

1 will start 2 are going to be 3 will establish 4 is going to replace 5 will know 6 are going to join 7 are going to send back

Let's aim high now! (page 58)

1 Next week they **will check/are going to check** the spacecraft carefully.
2 Next month scientists **will study/are going to study** soil and rocks from the moon.
3 Next Friday we **will visit/are going to visit** the observatory to learn about space.
4 Next year the spacecraft **will send/is going to send** information back to Earth.
5 Tomorrow morning they **will launch/are going to launch** the spacecraft if the weather is clear.
6 In the future, astronauts **will train/are going to train** for a long time before they go into space.
7 Soon, astronauts on the International Space Station **will conduct/are going to conduct** experiments.

Let's put it together now! (page 59)

1 were sailing 2 went 3 found 4 reached 5 send 6 will drill/are going to drill 7 will explore/are going to explore

Let's have fun! (page 59)

Verbs with the sailing ship—was discovering, saw, sank, landed, were trading, swam
Verbs with the motor car—travel, arrive, steers, speeds, stops, brake
Verbs with the spacecraft—will fly, is going to fix, will photograph, will record, are going to find, is going to explore

Let's have a test! (page 60)

1 Yesterday I watched a program about space exploration.
2 I will write a recount about Captain Cook tomorrow.
3 were hoping

4 sail
5 The spaceship reach Saturn.
6 They launched the spaceship next month.
7 are going
8 travelled

Unit 11 Ways of communicating

Let's find them! (page 61–62)

1 usually 2 occasionally 3 generally 4 verbally 5 easily 6 quickly 7 fluently

Let's go to the next step! (page 62)

1 away 2 carefully 3 afterwards 4 soon 5 clearly 6 upwards 7 excitedly

Let's aim high now! (page 62)

1 We arrived early for the performance. (When)
2 She waited tensely for her turn to speak. (How)
3 He phoned to say he would meet us later. (When)
4 The teacher gestured to him to move forward. (Where)
5 They ran inside when they saw the flash of lightning. (Where)
6 He moved his arms apart to indicate how big the fish was. (Where or How)
7 We clapped loudly to show how much we enjoyed the show. (How)

Let's find them! (page 63)

1 in 1876
2 across long distances
3 on your landline phone
4 through wires or cables/to the telephone exchange
5 into the mouthpiece
6 along wires/to your phone
7 in the earpiece/in the earpiece of your phone

Let's go to the next step! (page 64)

1 We've had this radio since April.
2 I sent a postcard to my aunt and uncle.
3 My brother got a mobile phone for his birthday.
4 We lost the signal on our television during the storm.
5 I made lots of phone calls to my friends this morning.
6 My cat walked over the keyboard while I was typing an email.
7 When I need information about something, I usually look on the internet.

Let's aim high now! (page 64)

1 on the roof
2 before/during/after the news
3 late at night
4 in/inside/at our house
5 over/across/down/up the road
6 from me
7 around/beneath/under it

Let's put it together now! (page 65)

1 daily 2 from 3 invisibly 4 through 5 quickly 6 instantly 7 across

Let's have fun! (page 65)

1 broadly 2 with on 3 perfectly at loudly
4 Long ago over

Let's have a test! (page 66)

1 She made the phone call earlier.
2 They are listening to the news in the car.
3 He announced the winner clearly.
4 quietly
5 by
6 to
7 until
8 between

Unit 12 Let's get creative!

Let's find them! (page 67)

1 with shady branches
2 from the tree
3 without a tail
4 on a branch
5 beside the pond
6 beneath the tree

Let's go to the next step! (page 68)

1 with 2 about 3 of 4 above 5 on 6 inside 7 in

Let's aim high now! (page 68)

1 with talent
2 on the walls
3 around that box
4 from the balcony/across the road
5 across the road/in the city

6 across the road/in the city
7 without an arm

Let's find them! (page 69–70)

1 one large box/a smaller box/the small box/ the bigger box/the big box
2 two toilet roll tubes/the toilet roll tubes
3 two plastic containers/the plastic containers
4 a glue stick
5 scraps of card or paper
6 the entire robot/your robot
7 an interesting face

Let's go to the next step! (page 70)

1 I might use those red beads in the blue box.
2 I kept the two little pictures from the exhibition.
3 Mum wove that pretty basket next to the table.
4 He liked the colourful border around my picture.
5 I am going to decorate that clay pot on the shelf.
6 Please pass me those long pieces of coloured wire.
7 She has written an exciting book about lost treasure.

Let's aim high now! (page 70)

1 A blacksmith made that iron horseshoe above the door.
2 Some of the sculptures in the museum are very valuable.
3 At the dog show, I saw a poodle with a fancy collar.
4 An architect designed that large house across the road.
5 My grandmother arranged the tulips in the tall vase on the dining room table.
6 I got my idea for that painting from a picture I saw in a magazine.
7 My mother has a beautiful necklace of precious stones that she wears on special occasions.

Let's put it together now! (page 71)

my about of An with curvy strands

Let's have fun! (page 71)

1 the old-fashioned painting in the fancy frame
2 the big circle in the top left-hand corner
3 the little girl with the crazy hairstyle
4 the modern statue between the two lamps
5 the scented candles on the table
6 a large can of green paint
7 a white rose from the bouquet
8 the old paintbrush without any bristles

Let's have a test! (page 72)

1 from
2 with
3 among
4 during
5 an
6 a large metal clasp
7 in the park
8 My uncle sculpted the tall bronze statue at the bottom of the garden.

Unit 13 The seasons

Let's find them! (page 74)

1 shorts, tee-shirts and thongs
2 school holidays, presents and fireworks
3 iced drinks, ice-cream and ice lollies
4 plums, peaches and juicy berries
5 Summer's
6 don't
7 can't

Let's go to the next step! (page 74)

1 This spring we won't be planting lettuce, tomatoes or spinach.
2 In the summer I'm going to swim, play cricket and go to the gym.
3 Gran says she'll knit me a jumper, a scarf and a pair of gloves for the winter.
4 Autumn's the time when the leaves on some trees turn red, gold and orange.
5 This summer we've seen lots of lorikeets, cockatoos and king parrots in our garden.
6 She doesn't know that the order of the seasons is spring, summer, autumn and winter.
7 They're still deciding whether they should go to Brisbane, Adelaide or Perth next summer.

Let's aim high now! (page 74)

1 **I'd** like to go to Japan in the spring, summer or autumn.
2 **They've** never been to a spring, summer or autumn festival.
3 She **doesn't** have skis, boots or goggles because she **hasn't** skied before.

4 It **isn't** as hot in Tasmania as it is in Queensland, Victoria or Western Australia.
5 **They're** predicting that the weather will be cooler, wetter and windier this summer.
6 You **can't** snowboard, make snowmen or have snowball fights if it **doesn't** snow in winter.
7 This autumn **we're** going to trim the rose bushes, tidy the flowerbeds and clean out the shed.

Let's find them! (page 75)

1 the bird **2** Dad **3** the dog **4** the dustbin **5** the smoke alarms **6** the outside doors **7** our bikes

Let's go to the next step! (page 76)

1 The men's job is to clear away the snow.
2 "I have found my sister's sunhat," said Cathy.
3 The children's winter uniforms are in the wash.
4 In spring the city's parks are full of colourful flowers.
5 The sun's rays are stronger in summer than in winter.
6 The students' swimming costumes were in their bags.
7 The cars' engines were overheating in the hot summer weather.

Let's aim high now! (page 76)

1 These winter pyjamas belong to Dad.
These are Dad's winter pyjamas.
2 This spring garden belongs to my friend.
This is my friend's spring garden.
3 That thermometer belongs to my teacher.
That is my teacher's thermometer.
4 This beach umbrella belongs to my cousin.
This is my cousin's beach umbrella.
5 Those snow skis belong to the young men.
Those are the young men's snow skis.
6 Those autumn crops belong to the farmers.
Those are the farmers' autumn crops.
7 These summer clothes belong to the ladies.
These are the ladies' summer clothes.

Let's put it together now! (page 77)

I love the colours of autumn, when many trees' leaves turn orange, red or gold. On our farm it's a busy season. We have to harvest crops, prepare fields for planting and move many of the animals into barns or sheds. The sun's rays aren't as strong as in summer, but it isn't cold yet. I like autumn because it is such a mild season.

Let's have fun! (page 77)

The snowman is wearing a hat, scarf and belt. He has a carrot for a nose and two black stones for eyes. The little girl's hair is short, and the two bigger girls' hair is long. We can't see their hair because it's hidden by their hoods. The tree's branches are heavy with snow, and the bird, squirrel and cat seem to be shivering.

Let's have a test! (page 78)

1 The four seasons are spring, summer, autumn and winter.
2 In winter I wear a thick jumper, long trousers and warm boots.
3 Who's going to summer school?
4 he had
5 This little boy's gloves are in his bag.
6 The child's paintings of autumn are on the wall.
7 The weathermans' predictions were correct.
8 The geeses' feathers keep them warm in winter.

Unit 14 Being adventurous

Let's find them! (page 79–80)

1 "I won't let you race on a BMX track," replied Mum, "so it would be a waste of money."
2 "Oscar and Grant have got BMX bikes," whined Nick.
3 "BMX racing is much too dangerous," said Mum.
4 "Not if you wear the right gear," persisted Nick.
5 "I've done some research on this, Nick," Mum said calmly.
6 "Wearing the right gear won't stop you from getting injured if you have an accident."
7 "I promise I'll be careful, Mum," said Nick.

Let's go to the next step! (page 80)

1 "What an adventure that was!" exclaimed the twins.
2 "How many adventurous things have you done?" asked my friend.
3 "Be adventurous and try something new," commanded the instructor.
4 "Some people are more adventurous than others," explained the man.
5 "The characters in this book have lots of exciting adventures," said Julia.

6 "Jasper is an adventurous boy," said his father, "so I'm sure he'll go on that ride."
7 "Being too adventurous can sometimes get you into trouble," warned my mother.

Let's aim high now! (page 80)

1 "One day I'd like to be a skydiver," said the boy.
2 Vera said, "My uncle is planning to climb Mount Everest next year."
3 "I prefer the safe sports to the more adventurous ones," said the girl.
4 "This summer we are going on an outdoor adventure," said Lin and Pat.
5 "What is the most adventurous holiday you have been on?" asked my teacher.
6 "Hang gliding, jet skiing and rock climbing are extreme sports," said Mr Evans.
7 Jarred said, "Scuba diving on the Great Barrier Reef is the most amazing underwater adventure."

Let's find them! (page 81)

2 It was fantastic to see them in their natural habitat.
3 They could expect hot, humid weather.
4 The sweltering heat wouldn't spoil their holiday.
5 She hadn't had enough time to see all the wonders of Borneo.
6 She would be returning there in the very near future.
7 It was the most adventure-filled holiday she had ever been on.

Let's go to the next step! (page 82)

1 was 2 could 3 had 4 were 5 found 6 took 7 was

Let's aim high now! (page 82)

1 he wouldn't try
2 my/his/her helmet wasn't
3 I/he/she/we/they needed
4 he was
5 he hoped
6 he/she would try
7 he/she was going

Let's put it together now! (page 83)

Rick's dad said he **will** would buy him a skateboard if Rick **promise** promised not to try any dangerous tricks.
"There's only one condition," said Rick's dad.
"You can't go to the skateboard park unless your mum or I are with you."
Rick said it **is** was a deal.

Let's have fun! (page 83)

"This is hard work!" exclaimed Natalie.
Natalie said that abseiling down was easier.

Let's have a test! (page 84)

1 "
2 ?
3 "We're going on an adventure!" Dad announced.
4 He said that I was riding my bike too fast.
5 would
6 were, was
7 "I wish I could go on an adventure trail." whined the little girl.
8 My friend said that she warns me it will be too risky.

Unit 15 What's making news?

Let's find them! (page 85–86)

1 Simon won 1000 boxes of jelly and he will be going to the World Jelly-eating Championships.
2 I might eat all of the jelly myself, or I might share it with my family.
3 I feel a bit wobbly, but otherwise I am fine.

Let's go to the next step! (page 86)

1 simple sentence
2 compound sentence
3 simple sentence
4 compound sentence
5 compound sentence
6 compound sentence
7 simple sentence

Let's aim high now! (page 86)

1 or 2 and 3 but 4 but 5 and 6 or 7 so

Let's find them! (pages 87–88)

1 The angry bird then turned on Mr Chu when he got too close to it.
2 We will have to get rid of the rooster because it no longer likes us.
3 Mrs Chu was so badly shaken by her experience that she is now terrified of all roosters.

4 If no one wants it, they will turn it into chicken noodle soup.

Let's go to the next step! (page 88)

1 unless 2 once 3 while 4 that 5 who 6 until 7 because

Let's aim high now! (page 88–89)

1 If you write the report, they will publish it.
2 Unless you start immediately, you won't finish the report.
3 Once he has read the magazine, he will give it to his brother.
4 Mum, who is an excellent cook, buys lots of food magazines.
5 George and I will write the story that we discussed yesterday.
6 The article that I read in the newspaper was about global warming.
7 I read the front page first because it contains the most important news.

Let's put it together now! (page 89)

1 that 2 so 3 If 4 but/although 5 who 6 because 7 but/although

Let's have fun! (page 89)

that
but
who
because
while
unless
once
which

Let's have a test! (page 90)

1 He writes articles for a magazine and she edits them.
2 but
3 or
4 I will read the newspaper and she will read the magazine.
5 The story, which was headline news, was in all the newspapers.
6 if
7 that
8 I heard about the earthquake that destroyed an entire village.

Unit 16 Secrets of the sea

Let's find them! (page 92)

1 After I had completed my scuba diving course, Mum and Dad bought me an underwater camera.
2 I was excited, but I was also a bit nervous.
3 In any case, Dad's friend Jim had been diving for years and nothing bad had ever happened to him.
4 The day of the dive finally arrived, with not a cloud in the sky.
5 By this time, the butterflies in my stomach were doing a war dance!

Let's go to the next step! (page 92)

1 On a scale from one to ten, I'd say that dive was worth a ten!
2 Some sharks, especially the very big ones, are truly terrifying.
3 To my great surprise, we saw more sea horses than clownfish.
4 At that moment, a huge octopus appeared from behind the rock.
5 By the way, those photographs you took of the coral reef are outstanding.
6 The fish, one of the most beautiful of its kind, was hiding amongst the coral.
7 Without a doubt, that was the most exciting underwater experience I've ever had.

Let's aim high now! (page 92)

1 If you spend too long underwater, you'll start to feel sick.
2 The fish, which is highly poisonous, looks just like a rock.
3 We saw lots of beautiful fish, but we also saw some ugly ones.
4 From where we were sitting, we could just see the wrecked ship.
5 While I was photographing the reef, a sea snake swam right in front of me.
6 Because I'd never seen a sea dragon before, I didn't know what I was looking for.
7 The boy, who everyone thought was an experienced diver, got into trouble underwater.

Let's find them! (page 93)

1 'The Little Mermaid'
2 'Treasure Island'
3 'Robinson Crusoe'

4 'Twenty Thousand Leagues Under the Sea'
5 'Finding Nemo'
6 'Shark Tale'
7 'Free Willy'

Let's go to the next step! (page 94)

1 My favourite TV program is 'Underwater Adventure'.
2 'The Diver' is a magazine that comes out once a month.
3 My father has written a book called 'A Guide to Underwater Photography'.
4 Jessica Watson's book about her experiences at sea is called 'True Spirit'.
5 I heard about the fishing competition on the radio program, 'Catch of the Day'.
6 She found information about the tides and weather in the magazine, 'Surf's Up'.
7 The young sailor was interviewed on the breakfast show, 'Good Morning, America'.

Let's aim high now! (page 94)

1 My brother's favourite film is 'Pirates of the Caribbean'.
2 A famous poem about the sea is 'The Rime of the Ancient Mariner'.
3 My father is working on a documentary called 'Tales of a Deep Sea Diver'.
4 Mum found a recipe for an unusual fish pie in the new edition of 'What's for Dinner?'.
5 My little sister's new library book is called 'Five Little Sharks Swimming in the Sea'.
6 Our music teacher has written a song called 'Pretty Little Seashells' for the school play.
7 The Australian television series, 'H2O: Just Add Water', is filmed at Sea World on the Gold Coast.

Let's put it together now! (page 95)

The afternoon started well. Mum was stretched out on a deck chair, reading the latest copy of 'The Australian Woman's Weekly'; Dad was waiting patiently for a fish to bite; Jackie was playing 'Popping Penguins' on Mum's phone; and I was slowly drifting off to sleep, lulled by the gentle movement of the boat. Then it happened. A squall, which seemed to come out of nowhere, whipped Mum's magazine right out of her hands. Jackie, who was sitting beside me, looked up in alarm. Dad told us not to worry, but I could see that he was nervous. That's when I felt the panic rise inside me.

Let's have fun! (page 95)

Title	Description
'Mermaids and Mermen: Myth or Reality?'	A book that questions whether certain sea creatures really exist
'Riding the Waves'	A magazine for surfers
'Giants of the Deep'	A TV program about the biggest animals in the sea
'The Ballad of the Sea'	A poem about the sea
'Hook, Line and Sinker'	A magazine for fishermen
'Treasures on the Ocean Floor'	A TV program about old shipwrecks
'Luxury Liners'	A TV documentary about ships that carry passengers
'Flippy and Flynn Go to Sea'	A cartoon for young children
'Captain Blackbeard Meets His Match'	A story about pirates
'Coconut Island'	An adventure story about a group of children who get shipwrecked on a desert island

Let's have a test! (page 96)

1 In the olden days, people didn't know much about the oceans.
2 again, I
3 I haven't been sailing yet, so I haven't seen many whales.
4 I have never seen a killer whale, but I know what it looks like.
5 The fish, which is extremely rare, is on show at the aquarium.
6 His new book is called 'The Call of the Sea'.
7 His new documentary, 'Predators of the Deep', is popular with viewers.
8 'Shark Attack'.

Notes